P9-EES-141

# Great Drivers,
# Great Races

# Great Drivers, Great Races

## by Howard Liss

J. B. LIPPINCOTT COMPANY · PHILADELPHIA/NEW YORK

U.S. Library of Congress Cataloging in Publication Data

Liss, Howard.
  Great drivers, great races.

  Summary: Discusses early racing history, such famous races as the
Indianapolis 500 and the East African Safari, and drivers such as Jim
Clark and Graham Hill.
  1. Automobile racing—Juvenile literature. [1. Automobile racing]
I. Title.
GV1029.L55                    796.7'2                    73-6656
ISBN-0-397-31278-4

FOR MICHAEL JED ROBBINS—
A GREAT RACING ENTHUSIAST,
AND AN EVEN GREATER FRIEND.

# Contents

# 1 · Early Racing

In 1680 the Dutch scientist Christian Huyghens managed to drive a piston directly into a cylinder. Since the world knew nothing of gasoline then, Huyghens used gunpowder. Thus began a series of step-by-step inventions that finally led to the modern piston-driven automobile.

A century and a quarter later, the Swiss inventor Isaac De Rivas duplicated Huyghens' feat, using hydrogen instead of gunpowder. To get some practical use of his device, he hooked it to a wheel and made the wheel move. Later, others experimented with the idea of turning a wheel through piston power. In 1860 the Frenchman Etienne Lenoir developed the first workable gas engine, using lighting gas for fuel. Lenoir went one step further, using an induction coil—a kind of electrical circuit—to ignite the fuel.

At about the same time Lenoir was experimenting, an Austrian named Siegfried Marcus tested benzene as a fuel, a giant step toward a more modern engine. By 1865 Marcus had put the ideas of many people together and built what is now thought to be the first gasoline engine. It had no brakes, no clutch, and could not change gears, but at least it ran over the roads.

By the late 1860s many inventors were tinkering with cars and engines. Among them were two Germans: N. A.

Otto, who invented the four-cycle engine (which was later improved and became the standard engine type for cars made in America); and his employee, Gottlieb Daimler, who constructed a really practical automobile in 1883. Daimler kept working on his ideas, constantly improving the engines. By 1889 Daimler engines were being exported to other countries. Soon the ranks of automobile engineers and builders were increased by such pioneers as Emile Levassor, René Panhard, Karl Benz, and the Frenchmen whose names have been associated with cars to this very day, Renault and Peugeot.

However, even before the engine could be installed in a car, first there had to be an idea called "the horseless carriage."

In 1769 a French army engineer, Nicholas Cugnot, designed the first vehicle of this kind. But it wasn't meant to carry passengers. Because the inventor was a military man, it was only natural that he should think of his brainchild as a device to haul field artillery. Cugnot called it a *fardier,* which comes from the French word *fardeau,* meaning "a burden." It ran on steam and it worked. Cugnot tested his machine by running it in a courtyard for about fifteen minutes, until it ran out of steam. Nothing much was done with Cugnot's first model, nor his second one, built a few years later. Rather than experiment with new devices, the French army authorities preferred to use animals to drag field pieces.

Since James Watt has often been called "The Father of the Steam Engine," it is only fitting that one of his assistants, a man named William Murdock, should try his hand at a horseless carriage run on steam power. In 1784 he built a smaller version of Cugnot's steam vehicle. Murdock's "automobile" had only three wheels, but the engine was more powerful. One night he decided to test it in the sleepy English village of Redruth. Somehow the machine got loose and rolled away, scattering sparks and hissing like a thousand snakes. The angry villagers made sure Murdock performed no more tests around their homes.

The idea of a steam-driven carriage had caught hold by then and others began to work on larger self-driven carriages. Among the inventors were two other Englishmen, Richard Trevithick and Andre Vivian. They constructed a kind of "bus" that could carry twelve passengers and rattle along at about nine miles an hour. However, the world wasn't quite ready for such advanced mass public transportation.

By then the notion of travel by "steam car" had spread to the United States. Some of the ideas incorporated into the newer carriages were quite advanced. In 1805 a man named Oliver Evans put on a demonstration that left people gasping in disbelief. He drove his steam car through the streets of Philadelphia and into the waters of the Schuylkill River. At that point the automobile wheels became paddlewheels and the vehicle began to move through the river like a Mississippi showboat.

It was probably in those days that the first "automobile races"—if they could be called that—were staged. Human beings have always liked to race, whether on horseback, in steam cars, or any other way. But the steam car races were not on an organized basis and no records were kept. It was all in fun.

Thus, toward the end of the nineteenth century, the horseless carriages were being driven by both steam power and piston engines. By 1873 steam buggies had already achieved a speed of 24 miles an hour, and a few years later that was increased to 27 miles an hour, while piston engines were still crawling along by comparison.

In 1888 a kind of liquid fuel was developed, enabling steam to be produced more quickly, making it unnecessary to wait a long time while boilers were heating.

Then a new entry arrived on the scene: the electric car. By the turn of the century, this "Johnny-come-lately" had reached the fantastic speed of 65 miles an hour! But, fast though it was, the electric car had a serious drawback. It could not run over long distances because the batteries gave out.

Soon even the electric car's speed was outdistanced by steam. In the early 1900s a Stanley Steamer broke every known record by streaking along at 197 miles per hour. True, the machine blew up, and only through a miracle did the driver, Fred Marriott, escape death. But that dash at more than three miles a minute seemed to end all arguments; steam was king.

Yet the piston engine refused to remain in second place. Many more improvements were made. And in its favor were two undeniable facts: piston-driven cars were less cumbersome and less of a fire hazard than steam cars. As the piston cars became better, steamers began to fall into disfavor. By the 1920s they had become museum pieces.

Disputes over the merits of steam and piston cars were one reason for the first automobile race. In 1894 the *Paris-Rouen Trial* was staged. Both types of cars competed. Although numerous accounts of that race have been printed, there is disagreement over what actually happened. One source has it that 21 cars were entered; another maintains that there were 102 entries and only 20 cars crossed the finish line. The true winner of that seventy-eight-mile race is also in doubt. One book states that a steam car driven by the Marquis de Dion won, with an average speed of 11.9 miles per hour. Another book claims that although de Dion's car did cross the finish line ahead of the rest, its speed was 11.6 miles per hour and, furthermore, de Dion was disqualified because he did not follow the regulations agreed to beforehand.

The idea of cars competing against each other in a town-to-town race caught on. It wasn't so much to see whether steam was better than piston; people were fascinated by the idea of *any* vehicle traveling so fast. In 1895 a much more ambitious event was staged; this time the race was from Paris to Bordeaux and back again, a round trip distance of 732 miles. And once again the real winner is disputed.

All racing histories agree that the race was open to cars of all sizes and horsepower. Nor is there any question about *most* of the rules. One rule permitted a change of drivers during the race, but it was optional. Emile Levassor, at the wheel of a Panhard, crossed the finish line ahead of the rest. Levassor drove all the way, stopping only for some quick snacks and a few winks of sleep. It took him forty-eight hours and forty-eight minutes to complete the round trip. His average speed was 14.9 miles per hour.

But Levassor was disqualified. Only four-seaters could qualify for the prize and Levassor's Panhard was a two-seater. The award was presented to a Peugeot finishing about six hours behind Levassor.

Auto racing as a sport captured the imagination of people all over the world. In the United States, the *Chicago Times-Herald* sponsored a town-to-town race between Chicago and the suburban community of Evanston, Illinois, and back, a round trip of slightly more than fifty-five miles.

On Thanksgiving Day, 1895, a number of electric and gasoline cars took off across the muddy, slushy Midwestern road. Before long most of the entries had dropped out; in fact only three cars managed to cross the finish line. The winner was Frank Duryea. He had to stop twice to make major repairs and it took him ten hours and twenty-three minutes to cover the distance.

By the beginning of the twentieth century, auto racing was established as a major sport throughout the world. New town-to-town courses were marked off in several countries. New drivers entered the field. Cars were made more powerful. Among the coveted awards to the winners were the *Gordon Bennett Cup,* donated by James Gordon Bennett, publisher of the *New York Herald;* and the *Vanderbilt Cup,* sponsored by wealthy yacht racer William K. Vanderbilt.

Through those early years of racing, the winning cars and drivers were almost always French. One year the British won "half a race," but somehow, when the final miles had been finished, the French still won. That particular event was the Paris-Venice Race, held in 1902. The Gordon Bennett Cup was to be awarded only for that part of the race extending from the start through to Innsbruck, Austria. It was unusual, but racing was still in its infancy then.

Speeding across the Alps, an English Napier, driven by S. F. Edge, passed a French Panhard. The Napier lost its brakes, but Edge kept the Napier going, maintained the lead across the treacherous 6,000 foot high Arlberg Pass, and managed to get to Innsbruck first to win the Gordon Bennett Cup section of the race. However, by the time Venice was reached, the overall winner was Marcel Renault, driving one of his own cars.

In the history of auto racing several individual years are turning points, when important changes were instituted. One such year was 1903.

By then the larger engines were capable of producing much greater speeds than even one year before. Unfortunately, the automobile experts seemed to forget about safety. The power plants, both steam and piston, were mounted on light frames that could not withstand the pounding over bad roads. Brake systems were shoddy. Steering linkage was poor. The cars could fly across the road, but the drivers were praying every mile of the way that their vehicles—and themselves, too—would be in one piece when the event was finished.

That 1903 Paris-Madrid Race was probably the bloodiest day in the history of sports.

The race began early in the morning, and the dim acetylene headlights did almost nothing to illuminate the road. Unable to see where they were going, several drivers had accidents just a few miles from the starting line.

Large crowds lined the dusty roads. Many people were curious about the new-fangled automobiles. Although police and soldiers were stationed along the course, many spectators slipped through the guarded roadsides to get a better look at the cars as they passed. They had no idea how fast the cars were traveling, and thought they could get out of the way without difficulty. The carnage that followed was awful.

Like human tenpins, individuals and groups of onlookers were knocked flying, many to their deaths, as speeding cars rammed into them. The racers smashed into small children trying to hurry across the road, they crunched dogs and other animals under their wheels. Some drivers, trying desperately to avoid hitting anyone, went careening into ditches or drove headlong into walls and trees and were killed. The failure of brakes, tires, and steering mechanisms caused additional fatalities and injuries. There was never an actual count, no one was sure exactly how many people were killed or maimed for life. It is known that there were hundreds of casualties—perhaps even thousands.

The race was never finished. It was called off at Bordeaux, some 342 miles from the starting line. A 70-horse-power Mors, driven by a French driver named Garbiel, was declared the winner with an average speed of 65.3 miles per hour.

The tragedy put an end to country-to-country races for a time. For the next three years only Gordon Bennett Cup races were held in Europe, all under strict government supervision. In 1907 there was another event crossing national borders, but the French government said nothing because it was more of a stunt than a race.

The editors of a newspaper, *Paris Matin*, sponsored a "race" between Peking, China, and Paris, France, a distance of not quite 9,000 miles. Five cars entered.

All preparations were very elaborate. The course was mapped out: starting from Peking, the racers went through Mongolia, then across the Gobi Desert into Siberia, over the Ural Mountains into Moscow, down into what later became part of Poland, then across Germany, Belgium, and finally western France into Paris. All along the route were depots stocked with tires, fuel, and other equipment.

The cars had to go through unbelievable obstacles and hazards, such as shallow streams, roads filled with holes and rocks—or no roads at all, through herds of animals, and, not the least, the glare of a cruel sun.

The race began on June 10, 1907. It was over on August 10. The winner was a four-cylinder Itala driven mostly by Prince Scipione Borghese of Italy. Three weeks later two other entries reached home.

The following year, *Paris Matin* sponsored another freak marathon, this time between New York and Paris. The cars drove across the United States to San Francisco, from there they were shippped by boat to Vladivostok, Russia. Then the course led partly over the same route as the previous race.

If anything, the New York-Paris race was even wilder than the previous round-the-world stunt. On numerous occasions the cars and drivers were almost smashed to bits. It was a journey through mud, snow, darkness, and trackless wastes. Six cars started the race on February 12. Five months and two weeks later, an American Flyer came in. Forty-five days later, the German Protos and the Italian Zust finished.

Meanwhile, American racing was developing in a more practical way. In 1903 a race was staged on a three-mile track at Grosse Pointe, Michigan. It was won by a four-cylinder, 80-horsepower car called "999." The two men responsible for that car have long since entered the automobile industry's Hall of Fame: the driver, Barney Oldfield, a former bicycle racer; and the man who built the car, a machine shop mechanic named Henry Ford.

The idea of track racing soon caught on. American roads were very poor in those days and racing was dangerous. But every fairgrounds had a good track where horses ran. Why not leave the horses in their stalls for a day or two and let the cars go spitting fire around the track? Fairground visitors thought it was a marvelous novelty.

In 1910 Charles G. Fisher, who built auto headlamps, got together with several other automobile executives and built an oval track on a piece of land outside Indianapolis, Indiana. It was supposed to be a kind of outdoor laboratory for testing automobile products. Since the track was then paved with bricks, it was given the name, "The Brickyard."

The first race at the Indianapolis track was held in 1911 and was won by Ray Harroun driving a six-cylinder Marmon. His average speed was 74.79 miles per hour.

European racing also began to develop in a more sensible way. Round-the-world races were merely stunts and did not prove which of the cars was faster or built better. Some excitement was lacking because racing enthusiasts had no one to cheer for. And most important, automobiles were becoming big business as manufacturers began to turn out cars in ever increasing numbers. Racing was a good way to test new engines and designs.

In 1906 the French decided to show the world that they were still masters of the road. And so the Automobile Club of France organized the *French Grand Prix* at Le Mans.

In some ways that race can be considered the start of modern road racing, for the entries were true racing cars, with open wheels and cockpits. Some sort of balance was maintained, for a vehicle was limited to one "long ton" (2,240 pounds). The race was run over a closed course consisting of main highways and back roads, all clearly marked. The cars had to cover twelve laps a day for two days, with a total distance of 1,238 kilometers.

As usual the cars developed the same difficulties. Tires were ripped, brakes didn't work, frames loosened, engines failed. But such malfunctions would happen, even in modern races. The French got some satisfaction because the race was won by a Renault. But it was driven by a Hungarian named Szisz. He averaged 62.8 miles per hour.

The French Grand Prix was a huge success. Over the years other Grand Prix races and courses were arranged in other countries. World Wars I and II halted competition, but only temporarily. After the fighting was over mechanics and drivers returned to their beloved sport.

As cars continued to improve it became evident that racing rules had to be changed. At first cars were little more than powerful engines mounted on skeleton bodies, because the less weight the engines had to pull the faster the cars could move. But then racing officials began to insist on more safety provisions for the drivers. Then the supercharger made its appearance.

Basically, a supercharger is nothing more than a blower device that forces more fuel into an engine than it would normally receive. That increases engine power. Therefore, an engine with a supercharger doesn't have to be as heavy or bulky, because the same horsepower can be attained with a smaller, lighter engine.

But superchargers "unbalanced" races. A heavy car without a supercharger was at a disadvantage, for the lighter car with a supercharger could attain the same horsepower. Yet some kind of measurement was necessary to equalize the entries in a race. The answer was *cc's* —cubic centimeters.

Imagine an open-ended metal tube. That is an engine cylinder. The piston, a round piece of metal, fits snugly inside the cylinder and is driven up and down inside the cylinder. The fuel is burned there.

Now imagine the space inside the cylinder, between the top and the bottom of the piston's stroke. That space is measured in cubic centimeters, which is a measure of *volume* or *capacity*.

In racing language there are several ways to describe this measure of volume. It can simply be called "cc's," which stands for cubic centimeters. Or, it can be measured in terms of *liters;* in European racing, one liter is equal to 1,000 cc's. In America the measurement is often referred to as *cubic inches;* one cubic inch equals $16\frac{2}{3}$ cc's.

To determine the power of an engine, all the cc's of all the cylinders are added up. It doesn't matter how many cylinders there are. It is possible for an engine with six cylinders to have as many cc's as an engine with eight cylinders.

Using cc's or liters or cubic inches as a unit of measurement, different formulas were worked out for various types of races. For example, it might be decided that in a certain race, no engine with a capacity larger than 3 liters, or 3,000 cc's, could be entered.

The *Fédération Internationale de l'Automobile* (FIA) is the governing body that makes the rules for all Grand Prix races. The *Commission Sportive Internationale* (CSI) is a kind of special committee of the FIA. The *Automobile Competition Committee of the United States* (ACCUS) is the American arm of the international governing body.

The formulas for different races have changed many times. Ordinarily, once a formula is agreed upon, it holds good for at least three years. But it doesn't always work out that way. For instance, in 1964 the Formula II events were changed from a maximum of 1,000 cc's to 1,600 cc's, after only two years.

Engine capacity is only one specification for cars in Grand Prix racing. Each entry must meet safety standards, including rupture-proof fuel tanks, roll bars, and safety belts. A Grand Prix race accepts only pure racing cars, which means open cockpits, open wheels, single-seats. Other specifications include the size and weight of the vehicle. All these cars are under the classification of Formula I.

There have been several different formulas for races. For example, Formula II was established years ago, for cars with smaller engines. To show how much a supercharger can increase engine power, at one time the limit for Formula II engines was 500 cc's for supercharged cars and 2,000 cc's for entries without superchargers.

In 1952 and 1953 all Grand Prix races were really Formula II events. But they were changed. Superchargers were outlawed and the limit on engine capacity was set at 1,500 cc's. Since that seemed to include Formula I, the two formulas were combined. At the same time *Formula Junior* was introduced, with a maximum of 1,100 cc's. Formula III was designated as having 500 cc's maximum. Also included was *Formula Libre*—Free Formula—where anything goes.

Although there are many other spectacular and important races, only the Grand Prix events count toward the coveted *Drivers' World Championship.* In 1950 a point system was devised, whereby drivers were scored according to how they finished in the Grand Prix series. First place counted 9 points, second place was worth 6 points, and then 4–3–2–1 through sixth place.

The first champion was Giuseppe Farina of Italy. He was succeeded by Juan Mañuel Fangío of Argentina, who won the title five times: 1951, 1954, 1955, 1956, and 1957. Albert Ascari of Italy won in 1952 and 1953. Other champs included Mike Hawthorn of England, Jack Brabham of Australia, Phil Hill of the United States, Graham Hill of England, Johnny Surtees of England, and Denis Hulme of New Zealand. They drove such magnificent cars as Alfa Romeo, Ferrari, Cooper, BRM, and others.

Another great kind of racing that does not count toward the Drivers' World Championship is the *Sports Car* events.

It is sometimes very difficult to define exactly what a sports car is. The engines are as powerful as Grand Prix cars, and in some cases even more powerful. The great drivers enter both types of races. But there are differences in the two types of cars.

A sports car is a two-seater, or sometimes it might have room for four. It is not open-wheeled. (The wheels are enclosed by some kind of "fenders".) While a racing car is designed especially to be one-of-a-kind and is practically put together, section by section, by hand, a sports car is really a modified production car. The FIA, which governs sports car racing as well as Grand Prix events, has established three general classifications: *Touring, Improved Touring,* and *Grand Touring* (GT), with several different engine sizes permitted. What does "production" mean, and how may these sports cars be "modified"? *The Sports Car Club of America* (SCCA) and *United States Auto Club* (USAC) have set up the rules.

The Touring Car is a production model, sold to the public for business or pleasure driving. It is not over four years old, and a minimum of 1,000 such cars must have been manufactured in twelve consecutive months. Only minor modifications may be made for a race.

The Improved Touring car is a car in current production. Some modifications may be made in suspension and the engine, but the brakes and carburetion cannot be changed.

Grand Touring are those cars driven in the important sports car races. GT cars may be built in limited quantities and have special body work, but they must also be available to the public. At least 100 such cars must have been produced in twelve consecutive months.

Although Grand Prix and sports car races have the most glamour, employ the greatest drivers, and yield the richest rewards, there are other types of auto races that are extremely popular. One such contest is the *Road Rally.*

Normally, a "race" means speed, but in a Rally, the key word is *control.* Actually speed counts for very little in a Rally.

A Rally course is laid out, and it can cover any distance, from a few miles to as many as 10,000 miles. The race can take a couple of hours to run, or it can take a month.

Rally cars are ordinary family cars which may or may not have special modification. For a difficult race, such as the East African Safari, special equipment may be added, such as heavy duty suspension, etc.

Each entry has a driver and a navigator. Not only do they have maps showing the route, but also they know *exactly* how long it should take to cover the ground. If it has been determined that the average speed of the race should be 45.9 miles per hour, that is precisely what the driver and his navigator try to achieve. The car coming closest to the predetermined time of the race is the winner.

In many ways a Rally is the most difficult of all road races because it requires so much pinpoint precision. In a normal race, three or four seconds can often spell the margin of victory when one driver finishes ahead of a rival. But in a Rally, a car can lose because it was driven four or five seconds too fast! Therefore, the navigator has a collection of special stop watches, odometers (devices which measure ground covered by a car), slide rules, and other gadgets, to keep him "right on the nose" or as close to the accurate time as possible.

Some Rallies—the easier ones—are actually community affairs, going from one town to the next. Nobody exceeds the speed limits. The course may lead through roped-off supermarket parking lots, down shady streets, over open highways, and across dirt roads. Others resemble the outlandish round-the-world races of the past, and they are almost as rugged. For example, the Round-Australia Rally is the one that is 10,000 miles long and takes a month to finish. The East African Safari requires four days and the course is 3,100 miles long.

Another type of competition that is popular in the United States, but somewhat less popular in Europe and other foreign countries, is the stock car race. These races are run under regulations set forth by the *National Asso-*

*ciation for Stock Car Auto Racing* (NASCAR) and the United States Auto Club. They spell out exactly the changes which can be made in a car. The vehicles are standard automobiles, such as can be purchased from any dealer. But many modifications are permitted to make the car safer and faster.

Other events, popular in various parts of the world, include the gymkhana (something like a zigzag slalom on wheels, involving the maneuvering of a car between pylons); midget auto races; economy runs; hillclimbing; and drag strip racing. Auto racing fans do not necessarily like all these events equally. But that is part of racing's appeal, there is something for everyone.

Of course, there are also the attempts to break the World Land and Speed record. The FIA governs that aspect of racing too. But it is so specialized that only a handful of drivers have ever attempted it. The record is determined by the highest average speed reached by a wheeled vehicle over a straight measured mile, from a flying start, in two runs. That means the car is flying at top speed when it zooms across the starting line, and continues for a measured mile before coming to a stop. Then the course is run again. The two speeds are averaged out.

This run is staged at the Bonneville Salt Flats, the dried-up bed of what was once Lake Bonneville in Utah. It is fourteen miles long and almost as wide. The cars—if they can indeed be called that—are practically guided missiles. Among the great names in this event are Sir Malcolm Campbell; his son, Donald; Dr. Nathan Ostich, the first driver to try for the record using jet power; Mickey Thompson; and Craig Breedlove. But these men are a breed apart, not competition drivers. They race against time, not against other vehicles.

Auto racing is by far the world's most expensive sport. Every year automobile manufacturers such as Ferrari,

Maserati, MG, Ford, Porsche, Jaguar, and others spend millions of dollars preparing new engines and body designs. The great drivers also earn enormous sums of money in purses and from endorsements of products. In 1969 the great Mario Andretti earned about a million dollars.

In every respect auto racing is faster, more dangerous, and requires more skill and courage than any other sport. Hurtling over roads at dizzying speeds, drivers weave in and out and ahead of each other, babying the brakes on tricky curves, knowing full well that sudden death might be lurking just around the next bend. The slightest miscalculation, a slick spot on the track, a snapped tie rod, an unexpected blowout, can send them careening into eternity.

Yet, in another sense, racing is like all other sports, in that the drivers of today know they owe a great deal to the heroes of earlier days, who blazed the trail for them to follow. It would require an entire book merely to list their names, but to cite only a very few is to honor them all:

"Hurrying Harry" Harkness, who won the first American driving championship in 1902.

Barney Oldfield, who won that pioneering oval track race in 1903. His name became a synonym for the word "speed."

Ralph de Palma, Earl Cooper, Peter DePaolo, Thomas Milton, James Murphy, Louis Meyer, Wilbur Shaw, and Rex Mays, all of whom won the Indianapolis 500 at least twice in the years before World War II, when engines and engineering knowledge were still crude by today's standards.

Achille Varzi, Louis Chiron, and Tazio Nuvolari, three of racing's greatest, were friendly rivals through racing's "Golden Age" of the 1920s and early 1930s.

This, then, is the story of some Grand Prix races, some sports car races, and a couple of Rallies. It is a world of its own, a world inhabited by men to whom speed and daring are a way of life. They live with death every time they get behind the wheel of a car. They know it, but try not to talk about it.

What is the secret of their success?

Incredible skill, thorough knowledge of engines and bodies and component parts of a racing car. A deep love for the sport. And endless hours of practice. How can anyone put that into a few words?

In a way one man did. Once Bill Vukovich was asked the secret of his success in the Indianapolis 500, which he won in 1953 and 1954. Vukovich thought for a moment and grunted:

"Always remember to turn left!"

# 2 · The Grand Prix

In the year A.D. 968 a Genoese family named Grimaldi acquired a section of land in southeast France along the Mediterranean Sea. Except for a short period from 1793 to 1814, the Grimaldis have always ruled there. The tiny principality is called Monaco, and most Americans have heard of the present rulers: Prince Ranier and his beautiful wife, a former American movie star named Grace Kelly.

Monaco is one of the most charming spots in all Europe, with craggy hills, a lovely horseshoe-shaped harbor, and very friendly people. At one time it was visited mostly by wealthy people who made the journey to the south of France to enjoy the warm climate, and to lose huge sums of money gambling at Monaco's fabulous Monte Carlo casino. Tourists and gambling are still the most important "industries" of the country. But since 1929, Monaco has also drawn many thousands of people who love auto races. The *Monaco Grand Prix* is one of the races that adds points toward the racing championship of the world.

In a number of ways the Monaco layout is different from all other race courses:

First, it is the shortest—only 1.9 miles per lap. But even that comparatively brief run is filled with the usual hairpin turns, zigzags, hills, and tunnels which make up the hazards of any course.

Second, it is undoubtedly the most scenic of any road race anywhere. True, the drivers keep their eyes fixed on the road, but if they did look away for a fleeting instant they could see from the top of a hill the many luxury yachts dotting the blue waters of the harbor, or catch a glimpse of the gambling casino or of the old-world pink-ish buildings or of the modern hotels along the waterfront as they roared by.

That brings up the third difference, which is the most unusual aspect of the Monaco Grand Prix. Nearly all such courses are laid out so that the drivers use public roads moving out of town and back into town. The Monaco race is run through the streets of the city of Monte Carlo. Many drivers think of Monaco as "going round and round the houses."

More than any other race, the Monaco Grand Prix tests a driver's ability to "thread the needle"; to see a momen-tary opening, to take advantage of it, and to pass another car. There are few straightaways over the course, none very long. Mostly, the drivers are fighting the wheel, tak-ing the turns, cornering, slipping from one side of the road to the other. A spectator once remarked that it was like using a powerful car to dodge through heavy traffic in a city street.

Then there is that tunnel, so bothersome that even the most experienced drivers tighten up as they approach it. The tunnel is dimly lit. Emerging into the glare of sun-shine causes a split second's loss of perfect vision. If an entry has stalled or spun out just beyond the tunnel, there is almost no time to avoid a pile-up. In 1950, the great Giuseppe Farina spun out as he emerged from the tunnel and was promptly hit by two other cars. More cars tore through and the crack-up chain began. By the time it was over nine cars were racked up—and the race had barely begun!

Sometimes an accident at Monaco can be spectacular and almost humorous—although there is nothing funny about a speeding car going of control. Once Albert Ascari lost control and his car veered, sideslipped, and rode right into the Mediterranean Sea. Fortunately, he wasn't hurt. But the splash looked like a geyser erupting from the water.

Yet the Grand Prix, the lovely climate, the scenery, and the gambling are not the only reasons racing enthusiasts flock to Monte Carlo. The old timers especially come to see the director of the race, the man who waves the flags and oversees the starting grid. They gaze in awe at the immortal Louis Chiron.

The 1920s and early 1930s are often called "The Golden Age of Sport." Baseball had its Babe Ruth, football boasted its Red Grange, tennis had its Bill Tilden, and golf was represented by Bobby Jones. They have all become American sports legends. In racing, the legend's name is Louis Chiron. Throughout Europe before World War II, people mentioned speed and Chiron in the same breath. Once a Czechoslovakian taxi driver, watching the flow of traffic zoom through the city of Prague, remarked to a visitor, "The trouble is everybody tries to drive like Louis Chiron. And there is *only one* Louis Chiron!"

The majority of racing drivers became interested in cars at a very early age—not Chiron. Born in Monaco, Chiron's grandfather was in the wine business, and his father was a maître d' in some of the most luxurious restaurants of Europe. When Louis was fifteen, his father was called into military service. Louis' mother had died earlier. A Russian princess hired the boy as a chauffeur and he actually learned to drive a car well by tooling around in a royal limousine. At the age of eighteen he too en-

tered the French army and became personal chauffeur to
Marshal Pétain and Marshal Foch. He liked the job so
much that he remained in service after the war was over,
driving for various French officers.

By the time Chiron was mustered out he realized that
his future lay in automobiles. At first he sold them, refit-
ting and reconditioning army surplus cars for civilian use.
Then, in 1924, he bought a sports car for himself and entered a hill climb. He won. And then he won a few other
races. In 1927 Chiron began driving under the sponsor-
ship of auto tycoon Ettore Bugatti. The victories mounted
steadily.

The magnificent duels between Louis Chiron, Achille
Varzi, and Tazio Nuvolari thrilled countless crowds. All
three were incredibly skilled drivers, but somehow it was
Chiron who captured the imagination of the people.
Driving a Bugatti, Chiron won Grand Prix races in Italy,
Spain, Germany, and France. At Monza, Italy, he bested
Varzi who drove an Alfa Romeo, and Nuvolari, driving
another Bugatti. At Nurburgring, Germany, he crossed
the finish line a full fourteen minutes ahead of the run-
ner-up Mercedes. In the French Grand Prix of 1931, Chiron teamed with Varzi to win the ten-hour race, covering
a record 782 miles.

Many, many times Chiron stared death down. Once, as
he was being refueled during a race, his car suddenly
burst into flames. Mechanics barely managed to pull him
to safety before the car and the entire pit became a blazing furnace. On another occasion, while driving at Monaco during a cloudburst, his car hit an oil slick and skidded into the sandbags. Five other cars piled into him.
Yet, three months later, he was back in the cockpit of a
car, racing in the German Grand Prix. A flying stone shat-
tered his windshield. Chiron lost control while moving at
140 miles an hour and went off the road.

Age didn't stop Louis Chiron, and neither did a new crop of magnificent drivers, such as Albert Ascari, Juan Mañuel Fangío, and the others who came into racing after World War II. In 1949, at the age of fifty, he won the French Grand Prix for the fifth time, and in 1950 he placed third at Monte Carlo behind Fangío and Ascari!

But no one drives forever and finally Chiron retired from active driving. Yet Monaco was his home; and what would the Monaco Grand Prix be without Louis Chiron in some capacity? So he became top dog, the man who gives the orders. Even the greatest drivers looked at him with awe as he gave the signals to start and finish the race.

For Chiron, for the spectators, and even for the cars and drivers, the 1964 Monaco Grand Prix could be called typical. The usual sixteen cars were entered, representing the great manufacturers. A record was set, and that wasn't unusual. No one was killed; in fact there had been no fatalities at Monaco since the race was inaugurated, thirty-six years before. The festivities were as colorful as ever. Recorded music blared from many hotels and apartment houses. Prince Ranier and his lovely Princess Grace were driven over the course in a 2.6-liter Alfa Romeo. Somewhat out of the ordinary was the group of pretty drum majorettes, twirling their batons and rapping on snare drums. And, as always, the spectators were out in force, filling the grandstand, massed on the hills, hanging expectantly out of windows along the course.

The drivers were out in force too. Pole position had been won by Scotland's Jim Clark, who had turned in the fastest practice lap, 1 minute 34 seconds flat. While Clark had not won at Monaco, he had already achieved multiple victories in the English and Italian events. In a few short years Clark would reach the heights as one of the greatest of all racing drivers.

One-tenth of a second slower was Australia's Jack Brabham, Monaco winner in 1959. Brabham had gone on from that triumph to win the World Championship title.

Third on the grid was England's Graham Hill, winner at Monaco the previous year. Hill had also won the World Championship title in 1962. Handsome, not very talkative, Hill was the kind of driver who wore out his opponents, hanging in, nursing his car along, picking his spots.

In fourth spot was Johnny Surtees, also from England. Surtees was destined to earn the Championship that year.

So the first four cars on the grid were in the capable hands of drivers who had won (or who would win) the World Championship at least once.

One of the more fortunate starters was Richie Ginther in eighth position. Only a short time before, Ginther's BRM was involved in a smashup at Aintree, England, and Ginther ended up in the hospital with broken bones and bruises. Patched up by the medics, Ginther had succeeded in running a lap in 1 minute 35.9 seconds over the snake-like Monaco course.

The race began under a bright, cloudless sky. The cars moved up, and the great Chiron dropped his flag with a crisp swing of his arm. It was a clean start.

The notables behind the wheels of their Formula I cars began to jockey for position. Jim Clark in his Lotus-Climax jumped into the lead immediately, chased by Jack Brabham, Graham Hill, Dan Gurney, Johnny Surtees, and Richie Ginther in that order. Clark went in and out of the tunnel leading by almost 200 yards, and was going just a shade too fast as he came to the *Chicane*.

Of all the zigzags in the course, the Chicane is by far the trickiest. It is a quick left-right turn. The left turn is made through a gate in a wooden fence. Once through it the driver has a sudden view of the beautiful harbor—but he doesn't dare look at the scenery because he must flick to the right. The cars are really moving at this point, generally swerving through the Chicane at about 110 miles an hour.

Clark slid momentarily across the road as he bounced off some bales of hay. Then, calling on all his great experience, he managed to put the nose of the car back on course. A nasty pile-up was avoided.

As Clark began to open his lead again, Gurney, tooling along in a Brabham-Climax, edged past Graham Hill's BRM. Then Brabham, also driving a Brabham-Climax, ran into trouble with his fuel injection system and waved Gurney to pass. Gurney took out after Clark, but the Scottish ace maintained his nine-second lead over the first few laps. Graham Hill was running comfortably behind.

In the ninth lap Clark's car suddenly began trailing sparks. The mounting of the rear anti-roll bar had snapped off the chassis and was scraping the ground. Driving ferociously, Clark clung to his lead lap after lap. But it was too dangerous. Had the whole bar come off it might well have hit Gurney, Hill, or some other driver. After the thirtieth lap Clark was waved to the pit. Oddly the trouble had almost corrected itself by then, for the bar had all but broken off completely and only one link was left. The repair job took exactly eighteen seconds, and Clark was back in the race; but now he trailed Gurney and the dogged Graham Hill.

Now some of the entries began to drop out. Johnny Surtees' Ferrari developed gear box difficulty. Brabham's fuel injection system began to act up, Trevor Taylor's car sprang a leak in its fuel tank. Dan Gurney, trying desperately to hang onto the lead felt his legs become a gooey mess from the oil leaking through his top fuel tank. By the sixtieth lap he was finished.

Fantastic! That was the only proper word to describe

Jim Clark's driving. Without the anti-roll bar the car handled differently and Clark adjusted. He was a mere five seconds behind the front-running Graham Hill, who was beginning to have trouble with his car too. Richie Ginther hung in there near the leaders, even though his clutch was all but gone.

Clark could take the pounding but his car couldn't. By lap number eighty he was blowing clouds of smoke, his gauge showing no oil pressure. He tried to keep on but it was hopeless. Graham Hill, handling his car so that it did not show what was wrong, had increased his lead to fourteen seconds and was opening the gap with each turn of the tires. On the ninety-sixth lap Clark's engine just quit half way up the hill. He got out and walked slowly back to the pit, an appreciative crowd cheering him.

Hill's car had no oil pressure either, but unlike Clark's Lotus-Climax the BRM, while perhaps not as fast, was somewhat sturdier. None of the other drivers realized Hill's difficulty. He kept the brave BRM limping along and finally it crossed the finish line. Second was Richie Ginther, an undersized chap with the heart of a lion. He had come through to finish behind the leader, his hands blistered, his cracked ribs tightly strapped.

It was a great day for Graham Hill, Richie Ginther, and BRM. For the second year in a row the cars had finished one-two. It was Hill's second successive win at Monaco. Car and driver had broken the course record, finishing in 2 hours 41 minutes 19.5 seconds. Hill and the BRM had set a new record for a single lap, 1 minute 33.9 seconds.

It is an old but true adage that records are made to be broken. Sooner or later a car and driver would break the 1964 marks set by Hill and the BRM. Fans at Monte Carlo did not have long to wait, one year to be exact.

In 1965 the average speed record, which Hill and the

BRM had set in 1963, was broken. The fastest lap record, also set by Hill and the BRM, was broken.

The holder of the new records was Graham Hill in a BRM, winner at Monaco for the third consecutive year!

## JIM CLARK

In almost every sport it is fairly simple to understand what makes an athlete great. A baseball player will hit fifty home runs or pitch twenty victories in a season, or steal bases constantly. The great football player throws touchdown passes, gains 1,000 yards in a season, makes impossible tackles.

But it isn't that easy to size up a great driver. Even the greatest don't win every race, or even finish in the money. Sometimes the car is at fault, sometimes it is the weather or track conditions, or perhaps it's a combination of many little things. Yet, in spite of the hundreds of things that can go wrong in a race, the great drivers manage to win their share, or they will finish second or third in a tough race.

Jim Clark was a truly great driver. No one can say he was *the* greatest driver of all time, because there is no such person. There have been many superstars of the road and track, and Jim Clark was one of them. Those who drove against him say so. Those who have watched him at Indianapolis or on the Grand Prix circuits say so. And even if they didn't, the record book says so. He was a winner.

Clark was born and brought up in Scotland's farming country. Like any youngster he was fascinated by anything with wheels and liked to drive the family tractor. During the years of World War II, while Clark was still very young, his father used a small Austin for transportation. Clark watched his father shift gears, operate the clutch and brakes. One day he sneaked into the car and put his observations to the test. And young Jim Clark succeeded in driving the car around the farm. He was only nine years old.

At the age of seventeen Jim got his driver's license, and his father gave him one of the family cars, a Sunbeam Talbot that had been driven only 12,000 miles. By then Jim was an avid racing fan, having read several library books, numerous motor magazines, and every bit of racing literature he could lay his hands on.

When Jim's family learned that he was entering Rallies, test meetings, and other small events, they voiced their disapproval. Actually, Jim's father was a prosperous farmer and Jim was expected to help with the planting, the sheep, and cows. Besides, the elder Clark was very upset because Jim was spending five times as much money on his car as it cost the family to run all the other cars. But Jim was determined to become a racing driver.

The early days of his career, while important, merely helped him to learn more about cars. He didn't win many races, but usually made a respectable showing. Clark was finding out how hard it was to drive, how dangerous. While he was still busy finding out about himself, feeling his way into the world of racing, he saw how quickly his friends could be erased by severe injury—or killed outright. Once, before a race at Spa, in Belgium, he was introduced to a driver named Archie Scott Brown. The next day Brown was killed when he skidded over a wet spot, hit a marker, and crashed.

Like so many others, Jim too had his brushes with death. He discovered how heat and a bad track can play havoc with cars and drivers. In 1961, in the French Grand Prix at Rheims, the heat melted the tar on the road and caused the gravel to work loose from the roadbed. As the cars rolled along, small rocks were flipped into the air. A few hit Clark, shattering his goggles and cutting his face.

By the end of 1962 Jim Clark was recognized as one of the best of the younger drivers. He had already won a number of important Grand Prix events, including the South African, Belgian, British, and Mexican. Some fans and drivers wondered how he would fare on an oval track such as the Indianapolis 500. They soon found out. In 1963 he placed second at Indy, a little more than thirty seconds behind winner Parnelli Jones. And 1963 was also the year Jim Clark won the World Championship of Drivers!

His driving that year stunned even the veteran racers as he ticked off one victory after another. Some opponents claimed that Clark won because his Lotus-Climax was simply the best car. Clark—and those who defended him—replied that all cars were good in a Grand Prix, and that sometimes his Lotus-Climax failed to last out the race for one reason or another. Sure, he was lucky, and that helped. But weren't the others often blessed with good fortune too?

Luck alone could not account for Jim Clark's winning streak from June 9 to July 20, 1963. In that space of time he entered four major races and won them all:

> The Belgian Grand Prix at Spa.
> The Dutch Grand Prix at Zandvoort.
> The French Grand Prix at Rheims.
> The British Grand Prix at Silverstone.

Sprinkled around the year were victories at Riverside, California; at Mexico City; at Monza in the Italian Grand Prix; at Karlskoga in the Swedish Grand Prix.

How about some of the races he didn't win? Almost always he was fighting for the lead when something conked out.

At Monaco he was forced to retire when the oil pressure was gone—but he was in the lead. At the Trenton State Fair a gasket blew. He was leading. In the Monterey Grand Prix, again he was ahead of the pack, until his oil cooler went bad and he was forced to quit. In the South German Grand Prix he finished eighth because of trouble with his drive shafts. But he had managed to set a lap record during the race.

When Jim Clark won the championship he was only twenty-seven years old, the youngest ever to attain that honor.

Nineteen sixty-four was an "also-ran" year for Jim Clark. Many drivers would have gladly settled for such an off year, but perhaps more was expected of Clark. He won the Dutch, Belgian, and European Grand Prix races, finished fourth at Monaco, fifth at Mexico. But his efforts were only good enough for third place in the championship ratings. Johnny Surtees won that year, winning the German and Italian Grand Prix races, placing second in the Dutch, the U.S. at Watkins Glen, and Mexico, and taking a third spot in the European. It was an excellent winning year for Surtees. Second among drivers was Dan Gurney with victories in the French and Mexican races.

Then it was 1965, another year, another try for the title. Everyone had stopped thinking of Jim Clark as just a lucky driver with the best car. No one can keep winning the Belgian Grand Prix year after year without great ability. Another great driver, fellow Scotsman Jackie Stewart, called the Belgian Spa race "perhaps the most dangerous road circuit in the world."

If anyone could judge a rugged course it was Jackie Stewart, for he won the World Championship in 1969.

During the 1966 Spa race Stewart flipped over and hung upside down in a ditch, unable to squirm out of the car. Graham Hill finally noticed his predicament. Hill stopped his car, walked to a nearby farm, borrowed a wrench, and, by taking off Stewart's steering wheel, was able to pry him loose.

The Spa Francorchamps course (that is its full name, but it is usually referred to simply as "Spa") runs through Belgium's Ardennes Forest. The road itself is a few miles north of the area where Germany and the Allies fought "The Battle of the Bulge" in World War II. What makes this course so dangerous? There are several reasons:

It is an ordinary road. When not used for the Grand Prix, it receives heavy use from trucks and passenger cars. The road is covered with dirt and grime.

There are eight corners on the course that are usually taken in fifth gear, meaning the car is moving anywhere from 150 to 170 miles an hour, more or less, depending on weather and road conditions.

The Burneville turn at Spa is one of the most dangerous in the entire series of Grand Prix bends. It is a right turn, located at the bottom of a long downhill straight. When it rains the foot of the hill turns into a kind of swimming pool. A car splashes into the puddle and is confronted with the change of direction. And if it hasn't rained, the road is still bumpy and wavery, so that maintaining control is a problem.

Yet in some ways the course "looks easy." It is very picturesque. The 8.76 mile lap leads through pine-covered hills, lovely meadows where buttercups grow in riotous profusion, and cool streams where sleek trout lurk under the banks. Sometimes a farm building sits close to the road and the bemused farmers watch, scratching their heads as the cars go blazing by. Perhaps that is why some drivers are lulled into carelessness and try to take the laps at an average of 130 or 140 miles an hour. That's when it gets dangerous.

For the 1965 race, practice days had been sunny and dry, but on race day it was overcast and a brief but heavy shower just before the race made the road treacherous in several spots. When the flag dropped and the cars roared off, the sprinkle of raindrops continued.

Graham Hill and Jackie Stewart were in the front row of the grid in their BRMs, as was Jim Clark in his customary Lotus-Climax. At the end of the first lap Clark led, his wheels kicking up a fine spray of mist. Hill was second, Stewart third, and behind them were Johnny Surtees in a Ferrari, Richie Ginther in a Honda, and Bruce McLaren driving a Cooper-Climax.

Slowly, steadily, Clark increased his lead. By the sixth lap he was slightly more than thirty seconds ahead of fellow Scotsman Stewart, and Graham Hill was far back. Surtees was finished by then because of a faulty valve. The rest were strung out.

Around and around they went over the steamy wet course. Some, such as Dan Gurney in a Brabham-Climax, Jo Rindt in a Cooper-Climax, and Lorenzo Bandini driving a Ferrari, were just trying to finish out the race, without even a prayer of winning. Gurney didn't make it all the way.

The rains came and went. The cars came and went. The race itself came and went. Jim Clark stayed in the lead, and at the end of the thirty-two laps he was still first. It wasn't a record. Clark had averaged 117.168 mph; five years earlier Jack Brabham had covered the course at an average speed of 133.630 mph. But—Jim Clark was the first driver to win at Spa Francorchamps for the *fourth consecutive year!*

The village of Silverstone is in Northamptonshire, a county in the southern midlands of England. During World War II it was a training base for RAF bomber pilots. When the war was over, the base was deserted, grown to weeds like so many other air bases in England.

Still, the Silverstone air base was in a strategic location, not too far from London and the cities and towns of the midlands. The Royal Automobile Club (R.A.C.) leased the former airfield from the British Ministry of Defense and turned it into a race course. Years later the lease was turned over to the British Racing Drivers' Club.

Once the British Grand Prix alternated between Silverstone and Aintree. In 1964 another racing course was completed at Brands Hatch. Since then the British Grand Prix has been held at Silverstone on odd-numbered years and at Brands Hatch on even-numbered years.

No course is ever easy, and Silverstone isn't a simple drive in the country either. The trickiest turn—Woodcote —comes just before the start-finish line, and almost every driver, at one time or another, has gone into a spin while trying to get around the bend. And there are other difficult twists and sharp turns in the course: Copse Corner, Naggots Curve, Becketts Corner, Stowe Corner, etc. However, the race takes just less than two hours to run, and the 100,000 spectators want more than that for their money.

So there are other races as well, such as one between big sports cars, another between old sports cars, and of course the practice runs by the Formula I cars days before the race. In time the course becomes oily and grimy. Slicks crop up everywhere.

In this 1965 British Grand Prix, Jim Clark's fastest qualifying time had earned him the pole position. But as the race started under leaden skies it was Richie Ginther in the Honda getting off the line first. Clark regained the lead soon enough, but Ginther hung in there in second spot through the first lap. He led by slightly more than a second.

Ordinarily, people think of a second as a mere tick of the clock. It doesn't amount to much in a two-hour race. But when cars are traveling fast and the single second is computed in distance covered, it takes on another meaning. For example:

Suppose a car is moving at 120 miles per hour. Every minute that passes, the car will have covered 3,520 yards. That is simple arithmetic. The car is whizzing along at two miles per minute and there are 1,760 yards in a mile. Divide 3,520 (1,760 × 2) by sixty (seconds in a minute) and the answer is not quite fifty-nine yards. Therefore, when Clark increased his lead to two seconds early in the race, he was leading by about 120 yards!

By the twentieth lap Clark was ahead by six seconds, and that took a bit of doing. The young Scotsman had set a new course record on the fifth lap, 1 minute 32.8 seconds. But Graham Hill, a perennial challenger in every race, had opened up his BRM and later in the race beat Clark's record by two-tenths of a second.

The dropouts began to fall away quite early. At the end of two laps Lorenzo Bandini's Ferrari pulled off the road with a blown head gasket. Ginther's Honda lasted only twenty-six laps (fuel injection trouble) while Denis Hulme in a Brabham-Climax retired after twenty-nine laps with a broken alternator drive belt.

Meanwhile, Clark had opened up a twenty-second lead. But now he was in trouble. The engine seemed to sputter and cough on the turns, indicating that the Lotus-Climax had a small oil leak. Clark babied the car by easing off the throttle going around the turns and picking up speed on the straights. By driving that way he hoped to save the engine. But then the metering valve in his fuel line also began to sputter and clank.

During the final ten laps of the eighty-lap race Clark's engine was popping and knocking louder than ever as the oil continued to leak out. Other cars were having the same problem, and the track was becoming dangerously slippery.

Graham Hill's engine was still in fairly good condition, at least it was better than Clark's. He took out after the front-runner, using all the experience and skill at his command. Slowly he began to knock precious seconds off the Lotus-Climax lead. By the final lap Clark's edge was less than five seconds.

By then Hill's car was giving the veteran driver fits. A bad master brake cylinder forced him to pump the brake pedal again and again going into every curve.

For Clark it had to be an all-out effort. Hill was coming on fast. No longer was the Lotus-Climax slowed going into curves. Oil leak or not, Clark took the bends with speed.

It was a chase right down to the flag. Hill tried doggedly but couldn't quite catch up. Clark zipped over the finish line barely two seconds ahead. One lap more and he surely would have lost.

But Jim Clark did win. It was the fourth time he had been victorious in the British Grand Prix. It was also his third successive win in a Grand Prix race.

If there is an "easier" course in Grand Prix racing it is at Zandvoort, home of the Dutch Grand Prix. There are a few turns which require the usual care, but also lots of nice long straightaways. Any difficulties are due to the terrain and the winds.

"Zand" is the Dutch word for sand. There is a lot of sand at Zandvoort, because the whole town is like one big beach. Actually it is a lovely resort area at the edge of the North Sea, outstanding for sunbathing and picnicking.

But when the wind starts to blow in from the sea, the sand comes with it. Even planting great stretches of grass and pouring in tons of black earth doesn't do much good. There's just too much sand everywhere.

So a strong wind can play havoc with a car trying to stay on the road. And the sand, spreading out on curves, can cause as much trouble as oil or ice.

For Jim Clark the Dutch Grand Prix was extremely important, for a win would just about wrap up his second Drivers' World Championship. He faced the usual tough competition: Graham Hill in the BRM, Richie Ginther in the Honda, Jackie Stewart in another BRM, Dan Gurney driving a Brabham-Climax, and all the rest of the drivers who worked the Grand Prix circuit.

Ordinarily, Jim Clark's racing strategy was simple enough. He liked to bolt out in the lead when the race started and then stay there until it was ended. It didn't work this time. Richie Ginther revved up the Honda and shot to the front. Graham Hill squeezed into second place. Jim Clark took his place in line. And at the end of two laps all three maintained the same positions.

But it was only a matter of time before the order was changed. It happened at the Tarzan Curve, which is practically a U-turn; the cars are going in one direction, and when they are done with the long curve they are going in the opposite direction.

Graham Hill, the wily British veteran with the handsome aristocratic face, overtook Ginther at the Tarzan bend by edging inside, then using the width of the track, moving from side to side to keep Ginther behind him. Then Hill bucked the wind with only one thought in mind: beat Clark! He wasn't worried about the second place Honda. It was the third place Lotus-Climax that posed the biggest threat.

Hill was right about the Scotsman. Clark almost—but not quite—caught Ginther on the next lap. He did it after the cars had gone around the course again. After that Clark set a new record of 1 minute 30.6 seconds for a lap, breaking the old record by almost two seconds. The previous record had been set the year before—by Jim Clark.

The streaking Scot took out after Hill, closing the gap. Clark passed the BRM just where Hill had passed Ginther, on the Tarzan Curve. After that the race was over.

In achieving his second championship, Jim Clark won *six* Grand Prix races in succession! To prove to the world that he wasn't just a great Grand Prix driver, that same year Clark also won the Indianapolis 500. No other driver, past or present, could boast such a record.

Early in April of 1968 Jim Clark went to Hockenheim, Germany, to take part in a Formula II race. It was supposedly just one more race for the Flying Scot.

During the early part of the event, coming out of a turn called Shrimp's Head and into the straightaway, Clark's gold and red racer suddenly veered sideways. At 175 miles an hour the car slammed into the woods and smashed against a tree. The main impact was exactly where Jim Clark was sitting, strapped inside the open cockpit. He was killed instantly.

How great was Jim Clark? What heights would he have reached had he lived longer, to add more victories to his illustrious career? It is difficult to judge such things. But some comparisons can be made, to evaluate Jim Clark's record against that of another great driver, Juan Mañuel Fangío.

Fangío won the World Championship five times, four of his titles coming in succession (1954–57). Clark won the championship only twice. But in eight years of Grand Prix racing Fangío scored twenty-four major victories. Clark had twenty-five wins, and he did it in seven years.

Actually, it took Jim Clark only six years to win two dozen Grand Prix races (the same number as Fangío won in eight years); in 1961 he had won only one Grand Prix, the South African.

How did other drivers feel about Jim Clark's fantastic skill behind the wheel? Richie Ginther, who had been forced out early in the 1965 Silverstone event, watched closely as Clark jumped out into the lead and kept babying his stricken Lotus-Climax as it leaked oil. Ginther saw Clark use every trick known to racing—and a few moves he invented as he went along—to keep Graham Hill from overtaking him. Ginther grunted and muttered, "I can see why Clark is the best driver in the world."

## MEXICAN GRAND PRIX

Every race, whether it is a Grand Prix, a sports car epic, or a rally event, has its own particular challenge. Sometimes the difficulty lies in the rugged course, such as Nurburgring. Le Mans poses problems because it lasts twenty-four hours. The Indianapolis 500 presents a pair of challenges in the distance to be covered and the heat out on the track.

The Mexican Grand Prix is held at a sports park on the outskirts of Mexico City. The 3.2-mile track is tricky enough, with its fast straights, hairpin turns, and S-shaped squiggles. It gets hot enough on the track. But the most bothersome thing of all about the race is the altitude. The circuit is situated 7,400 feet above sea level. The air is thin. Human beings get tired quickly in the rarified atmosphere. Working, running—even walking—become difficult.

Odd though it sounds, on this circuit racing cars "get tired" too. The engine has trouble "breathing" and one of the big mechanical problems is getting just the right mixture of air and fuel. Pit men say that cars must sacrifice about 20 percent of their power because of the thin air, and tires have about five pounds less pressure. Cars never perform at peak efficiency. Neither do drivers.

However, since 1963 the Mexican Grand Prix has counted toward the Drivers' World Championship and the Car Constructors' Championship (which is to manufacturers what the Drivers' title is to a race driver). So the usual array of men and cars comes to Mexico City, and all are thankful that the Mexican event is the last of the championship Grand Prix races for the year.

Because it is the last one, the Mexican Grand Prix has decided the World Championship on a couple of occasions. In 1964 the issue was between Graham Hill, Johnny Surtees, and Jim Clark. If Hill won, obviously he would be the champion because he was leading in the point total. If Surtees won, he would be the champion even if Hill came in second. In order for Clark to become champion, Hill would have to drop out before the finish and Surtees would have to place no higher than third, while Clark himself won the race.

As it turned out none of them won the Mexican event. By finishing second, Surtees gained the championship. Clark came in fifth and Hill was eleventh. So Hill was second in the championship standings, Clark was third, and Richie Ginther tied with Lorenzo Bandini for fourth place.

In 1967 two drivers, Jack Brabham and Denis Hulme, went right down to the wire. Oddly enough Brabham was Hulme's employer! If Brabham (the "boss" driver) won and Hulme came in fifth, Brabham would win the championship. Actually, they would be tied in total points, but Brabham would be declared the champion because he had won three Grand Prix races (France, Canada, and now Mexico) while Hulme would have won only two (Monaco and Germany).

Hulme took no chances on losing the precious World

Championship. He fell into position behind Brabham and never let the boss get away. It was a dull race—Jim Clark won it—and Brabham finished second, while the dogging Denis Hulme came in third and took the year's honors.

It was a tough one for Brabham to lose, but he had won the championship the previous year (and twice more besides). Hulme deserved the cup.

On the other hand, little Richie Ginther went into the 1965 Mexican Grand Prix without ever having won a major race. Of course he had won a lot of other races, but never a Grand Prix. He had been racing about six years then. The car he was driving, a Honda, had also been shut out of first-prize Grand Prix money.

Paul Richard Ginther certainly didn't look like a race driver. At five feet five inches tall and weighing about 130 pounds, he looked like an overweight jockey. Richie had been sickly as a boy; his heart murmur had kept him out of athletics.

In 1946, when Richie was about sixteen years old, he met veteran race driver Phil Hill, and that was also his introduction to auto racing. The two Californians became fast friends. Richie knew and liked engines. His father was an aircraft worker, and later, after he was graduated from high school, Richie also worked in an airplane plant. In fact when Richie was in Korea during that war, he was a helicopter engineer.

But his greater love was cars. Phil Hill let Richie help out in the pit once in a while. Sometimes he drove, assisting Hill with his Ferrari. In 1960 there was an opening for a driver when Dan Gurney left Ferrari, and Richie joined the team.

Richie didn't do too well in his first race, which happened to be the Targa Florio. He crashed into a tree. But in his first Grand Prix race he did a lot better, coming in second at Monaco.

Perhaps Richie Ginther's failure to win was due to the fact that he never got the best car a manufacturer entered. Somebody else was given the cream. Yet everyone agreed that he knew more about engines than most other drivers. He seemed more "tuned in" to a car while it was running; he understood every stroke of the pistons and sensed when something was going wrong.

For the 1965 Mexican race Richie finally did have his choice of cars. Honda, for whom he was working by then, had sent two cars to Mexico City. Richie would drive one and an able young driver named Ronnie Bucknum would handle the other. During the practice sessions Richie went from one car to the other, testing, tinkering, monkeying around, setting up the cars in turn the way he wanted them. That made things tougher for Bucknum. But Ginther had been in that position before he became head man. Now at last he could tune the cars the way he thought best.

Eighteen cars were on the starting grid at race time, but all were not the best of each manufacturer. Several cars had been eliminated during practice. Jim Clark's Lotus-Climax practically exploded and he was given another one. Pedro Rodriguez lost a wheel. Jo Bonnier's Brabham-Climax suffered a break in the chassis.

However, that didn't mean the cars they were driving were poor or not capable of making a good showing. Indeed, in making a run for pole position in the "second" Lotus-Climax, Jim Clark broke his own track record by a full second! Richie Ginther was in third spot. Ronnie Bucknum in the other Honda started tenth.

As the race began Ginther seemed hardly to be moving. Car after car shot by him and he seemed quite worried. Then, suddenly, the Honda came alive and Richie zoomed away with a motorcycle roar. At the end of the first lap he was well in the lead, trailed by Jackie Stewart in a BRM, Mike Spence in a Lotus-Climax, and Dan Gurney in a Brabham-Climax.

Jack Brabham stopped being a threat early when his car blew a gasket. Before the tenth lap was done Jim Clark became a spectator rather than a racer because his engine quit. Later on Jackie Stewart's clutch stopped working, Lorenzo Bandini cracked up, and Pedro Rodriguez's battery went dead.

Meanwhile, Ginther stayed in the lead and even opened the gap wider. But it wasn't easy. The Honda's fifth gear kept acting up; it just slipped out. Things got so bad that Ginther had to hold the gear lever in place with his hand, and even then the stick sometimes jumped out of its slot. As the race wore on he developed a sore, blistered right hand.

As the race wound down to its final laps only Dan Gurney had a chance to overtake Ginther. Slowly he began to close the distance between them. Gurney would gain two seconds, only to lose a second back on the hairpin. Then he would regain the lost second on the straights.

Gurney never did catch Ginther. Richie drove a beautiful race, timing his moves splendidly. By the time Gurney was moving into the hairpin turn Ginther was just leaving it. And the Honda might have inched out even farther ahead, but that fifth gear wasn't working properly. Ginther took the flag just two seconds ahead of Gurney.

Only eight cars finished the race and almost none were in condition to go much farther.

Not only had Richie Ginther finally broken into the big-time winner's circle, but so had Honda. Furthermore, both Hondas managed to finish the race; Ronnie Bucknum came in fifth.

# 3 · Sports Car Races

It has been said that an automobile race can be divided into two parts, both of which are happening at the same time. The first part is between the individual cars and their drivers, each trying to finish ahead of the other. The second part of the race is a grim contest between all the drivers and the course they are running. Every driver is trying to get around the route a little faster than the last time, trying to master the tricky turns and straights. Cars and drivers usually take a beating, and sometimes they do not survive. But the course remains, ready to take on a new crop of contestants the next time there is a race. One of the best examples of a difficult course challenging the best drivers is Sebring.

When World War II ended, auto racing began making a comeback in Europe. In the United States it was really just beginning. Few American cars were entered in overseas races. Nor were there very many tracks in the United States. The majority of the famous tracks and courses in America have been built since World War II.

Race tracks have often been built in the unlikeliest places, and Sebring was one of the most out-of-the-way places of all. Originally, the site had been a B-17 bomber training base in the central section of Florida, a few miles north of Lake Okeechobee, the state's largest lake. The

51

old base was a maze of airplane runways and service roads. It was converted into a race course as a kind of American version of France's great Le Mans endurance contest. In some ways the races are alike, in others they are not.

All kinds of sports cars compete at Sebring, the same as at Le Mans. Big 400 horsepower cars must find their way around little Austins and Alpines and Sprites. For years there was a Le Mans-type start at Sebring, with drivers sprinting to their cars, starting up, and zooming away. But that has been stopped.

The differences include the time of the race and the type of course. Le Mans lasts for twenty-four hours, Sebring for only twelve. Le Mans' course has tunnels, dips, bridges, and other difficulties. Sebring, on the other hand, has been described as "a series of drag strips connected by turns." The 5.2-mile track, with its pretzel-shaped route has ruined more brakes, more tires, more gearboxes than almost any other in racing.

Imagine whipping along one of those nine-tenths-of-a-mile straightaways at more than 150 miles an hour. Then the gears must be muscled down in a double downshift in order to slow to 30 or 40 miles an hour for a hairpin curve. As the brakes are stomped, gearboxes grunt, outraged tires squeal and scream, the car skids and sways. Then comes another short straight and the car jerks ahead, the speed indicator climbing past the 100-miles-an-hour mark in seconds. The straights and curves come with bewildering swiftness and the feet hop around from brake to throttle. It's crazy!

Florida's unstable March weather is also a factor in the Sebring race. At eleven o'clock when the event begins, a searing early spring sun may be beating down 95 degree heat, baking the course—and the spectators—to a nice crisp. Then a sudden storm may blow up, drenching the track, the drivers, and spectators, and blowing litter everywhere.

Yet most drivers consider Sebring a relatively safe course. Perhaps it is because there have been comparatively few fatal accidents and most of them have been freaky. Once a driver tried to avoid hitting a local photographer who had foolishly stationed himself in one of the escape roads. The driver lost control, hit the photographer, swerved, and crashed. Both were killed.

On another occasion Mario Andretti, one of racing's most sure-handed drivers, tried to shift down from fourth gear to third. Something went wrong and the car was rammed into first gear. At that time Andretti had just passed Don Webster's Porsche. The timing and wrong gear proved tragic.

Jerked to an unexpected slow speed by first gear, Andretti went into a wild spin, zigzagging all over the track. He was so busy fighting the wheel that he didn't feel Webster's car hit him. Webster had lost control. The Porsche ricocheted into a group of people who had been standing dangerously close to the track. Four of the spectators were killed, although Webster suffered only minor injuries. Andretti was able to bring his car into the pit, but when he tried to restart it, the car—a Ferrari—burst into flames. Andretti barely managed to get away.

There have been some accidents which might have happened in any race. One involved Canadian champion Bob McLean. His Ford GT skidded on a hairpin turn. The car slid over the sand, bounced up over the curb, sheared off a pole, and exploded. McLean never had a chance.

Like Le Mans, Daytona, and other endurance races, Sebring is a difficult race to predict. Some great drivers have entered for years and never won either at Sebring or Le Mans. Other drivers have won both races handily.

For instance, Phil Hill has taken the flag three times at Le Mans and three times at Sebring. Olivier Gandebien has won four times at Le Mans and three times at Sebring, in fact on several occasions in those victories his partner was Phil Hill. Ludovico Scarfiotti has won both races and so has the team of Jackie Oliver and Jackie Ickx.

But relatively unknown drivers have also done well at Sebring. In 1970, the Revson-McQueen team stayed in the running until the final bitter laps, losing out by a surprisingly small margin. Peter Revson, heir to a cosmetics fortune, had already begun to make a name for himself as a driver and his good showing was not altogether unexpected. However, his partner in this instance happened to be movie star Steve McQueen. Probably the average fan had forgotten that McQueen was once a motorcycle racer. He proved his driving ability by turning in some creditable laps, even though one of his legs was in a cast!

Racing officials once frowned on the idea of women competing in a rugged endurance race. But the 1967 Sebring event had four teams of women. The men passed the usual remarks and made a few unfunny jokes. But, aside from the fact that traditionally racers have been men, there is really no reason why a woman cannot drive in a race. Certainly a woman's reflexes are as quick and as sharp as a man's. A race such as Sebring is grueling, that is true; but anyone in good physical condition can stand the strain. And size certainly has nothing to do with a driver's ability. The best example of that was Mario Andretti, a little man who was slated to drive a Ford Mark IV in the 1967 race.

Standing about five feet five inches tall and weighing somewhere in the neighborhood of 135 pounds, Andretti looked as if he would topple over under a stiff wind. Yet no one was more admired and respected than this little guy with the determined look on his face.

Mario Andretti was born in 1940 in northern Italy, near the city of Trieste. His father was an important man in the agricultural administration. During World War II the family lost everything. The Andrettis went to live in Florence, and in 1958 migrated to Nazareth, Pennsylvania.

Mario and his twin brother, Aldo, were automobile fanatics even before they were teen-agers. They idolized European (and later American) drivers, and the boys liked to hang around garages, talking to the racers, watching cars being tuned up. They had one abiding dream, to become Grand Prix drivers. Without telling their parents, the boys entered a driving program especially set up for young people. Mario and Aldo tasted competition at a very tender age.

Aldo never did achieve stardom but Mario did. He learned his craft well, driving jalopies, midgets, and sprint cars on dirt tracks. Mario took chilling risks, looking for the smallest opening to squeeze his car through, taking turns short when he thought there was a chance to bypass an opponent.

By 1965 Mario Andretti had enough of a reputation to enter the Indianapolis 500. He promptly set a record for a qualifying lap, and he finished third in the race.

The following year Mario was again part of the Indy scramble. He jumped out into the lead and threatened to stay there. But it wasn't to be his day. After only sixty-eight miles a valve broke and he was out of it.

If Mario couldn't win at Indianapolis those years, he certainly could take the flag elsewhere. In 1965 he won at Raceway Park, Indianapolis (*not* the famous 500-mile race; this was a 150-mile paved road course). In 1966 he won at Milwaukee, Langhorne, Atlanta, plus the Hoosier Hundred at Indy Fairgrounds, at Trenton, and at Phoenix. These races ranged in length from 100 miles to 300 miles, and were run over paved-mile oval tracks, over dirt-mile oval tracks, and paved road courses.

Co-driver with Andretti in the 1967 Sebring event was Bruce McLaren, a steady, keen-eyed man from Aukland, New Zealand. McLaren became a race driver because of an accident, but it wasn't with a car. When he was a youngster he fell off a horse and as a result of the bad spill the growth of his left leg was stunted. When McLaren left the hospital he walked with a limp which stayed with him the rest of his tragically short life. His father owned a garage-service station, and for therapy he gave the boy an Austin sports car to drive. Bruce took to cars naturally. In an amazingly short time he was one of New Zealand's best sports car drivers.

In 1958 the New Zealand International Grand Prix Association began a program intended to develop the talents of their own drivers. They sent the best young men to Europe so that they could get a taste of big-time racing. Bruce McLaren was the first to be chosen.

In Europe McLaren met Australian Jack Brabham, who was destined to win the Drivers' World Championship in 1959, 1960, and 1966. At that time Brabham was driving for Cooper, and he helped McLaren get a ride in a Cooper Formula II car.

Bruce McLaren remained in the shadow of Brabham for a long time. He never racked up a great record as a Grand Prix driver because he was much more interested in sports cars. Besides, he had his own dream—to head up a team of drivers for a car company. By 1966 he was with Ford, and he did well for them. With co-driver and fellow New Zealander Chris Amon, he won the 1966 Le Mans classic and seemed well on his way to greater things as the head man of "Team McLaren."

In the minds of many experts, Sebring 1967 boiled down to a race between Ford and its arch rival, Ferrari.

After some frustrating races when the American cars kept losing, Ford finally came back strong. After the 1966 Le Mans victory over Ferrari, Ford was confident it could repeat history at the Daytona track in February of the following year. But Ferrari turned the tables, sweeping Ford right out of contention. Stung, the Ford engineers went back to the drawing boards. They were certain that their Mark IV entries would avenge the humiliation of Daytona, and Sebring was the place to do it.

But Ferrari ducked the Sebring confrontation, preferring to concentrate on Le Mans, which would come up three months later, in June. There were Ferrari cars entered at Sebring, but not an official Ferrari team of drivers.

So Sebring 1967 shaped up as a contest between Ford's Mark II and IV series and another arch rival—Chaparral, sponsored by Chevrolet. The guiding hand behind Chaparral was a Texan named Jim Hall. The big brain behind many of the Ford racing cars was another Texan, named Carroll Shelby. That day in 1967 there would be another difference between the two Texans, besides their opposing cars. Shelby had given up driving some years ago; but Jim Hall was forced to get behind the wheel because Phil Hill, who had been scheduled to co-drive with Mike Spence, was rushed to the hospital with appendicitis.

The race went almost as expected; it was a duel between Ford and Chaparral. After some jockeying around during the first lap, McLaren took the lead with two Chaparrals nipping at his heels. The New Zealander stayed out ahead for almost an hour and a half, until he rolled into the pit to be relieved by Andretti. The second-place Chaparral, its airflow wing above the car's tail gleaming in the hot sun, swept ahead. Andretti got out onto the track and the duel continued. Sometime during his first turn at the wheel Andretti set a lap record, slightly more than 109 mph.

As the grind went on, engineers began to note the differences between the candy-yellow Ford and the bone-white Chaparral. The Ford was drinking fuel thirstily, getting only eighty to eighty-five minutes per tankful. On the other hand the Chaparral, with its automatic transmission, was burning huge gobs of oil, something like seven quarts on each pit stop. Overall, the Ford would have to make more frequent pit stops than the Chaparral.

Still these two cars fought it out. Ford's record fell when the Chaparral set a new lap speed of 111.032 miles per hour, and that was the fastest lap of the day.

Other cars dropped out through the day. There was a collision between a Porsche and a Ferrari, mechanical difficulties in a Corvette; and more cars quit for one reason or another.

At the height of the afternoon the weather began to bother the drivers. Out on the track the heat was oppressive, but the constant wind made the cars jump and buck and sway dangerously.

A little more than six hours after the race began, the wheel-to-wheel fight between Ford and Chaparral came to an end. Hall's car began to puff out smoke. Slowing, it staggered into the pit, where the trouble was diagnosed. The seals on the automatic transmission had broken. It would take practically forever to repair. The Chaparrals were finished.

Now it was just a matter of hanging on. Andretti and McLaren didn't dog it, but neither did they take unnecessary chances as they drove to victory. A Ford Mark II, driven by the team of A. J. Foyt and Lloyd Ruby, gave Ford some anxious moments. In fact the Mark II was in the pit when the race ended. But it had completed enough laps at the end of the twelve-hour grind to be counted as the second-place finisher. Third was a Porsche.

As for the women, they did all right, finishing seventeenth, twenty-third, and twenty-fifth.

After it was over, Ford officials talked about their chances for a real victory over Ferrari in the forthcoming Le Mans event, team against team. They knew it would be a tough one. Thoughtfully, Mario Andretti said, "We knew all along the Mark IV had it. We knew it would run the distance. And I promise you, it's just made for Le Mans."

About three months later, Ford, Ferrari—and the world of racing—all found out together.

## THE TWENTY-FOUR HOURS OF LE MANS

Ordinarily, the average sightseer in France would have little reason to visit Le Mans. Outwardly, it is not very different from a number of similar towns throughout France. Situated about 130 miles southwest of Paris, Le Mans factories produce textiles, chemicals, machinery, and shoes. The Sarthe River wanders through the peaceful countryside, which is dotted with tobacco farms. A chance visitor would probably be interested in the town's old Roman ruins, or the Cathedral of St. Julian, built in the eleventh and twelfth centuries.

But for those who love fast, well-built sports cars, Le Mans is the greatest spot on earth—practically a shrine. During one weekend in June, hundreds of thousands of racing fans pour into the area, filling nearby inns and boarding houses to overflowing, jamming the cafes and restaurants. They have come to witness the toughest, most demanding automobile race of all, a marathon endurance contest popularly called *The Twenty-four Hours of Le Mans.*

In many ways the Le Mans race is different from any other race between automobiles. For one thing it lasts a full twenty-four hours, starting at four o'clock in the afternoon and ending at four o'clock the afternoon of the following day. The cars keep going throughout the entire twenty-four hours, stopping only for fuel, swift repairs, or a change of drivers.

Naturally, speed is important in any race, but in the Le Mans event a car's stamina and construction are even more vital. Can it take a high-speed pounding hour after hour, mile after punishing mile? On the average, a winning entry at Le Mans will have traveled between 2,700 and 3,200 miles in that single day, or roughly the distance between New York City and Los Angeles, California. Every inch of metal, every scrap of rubber in the vehicle will be chewed and beaten before the race is done.

Perhaps machines can take such a terrific beating and come through the ordeal, but men cannot. Throughout the race a driver is constantly shifting gears, applying slight pressure to the brakes, stepping down on the accelerator, moving in and out of curves, threading through other cars. It is difficult enough during the daylight hours, but at night it is much, much harder. Quite often a fog will roll in, or the rains will wash down in blinding sheets. Anyone who has driven an ordinary passenger car at night under such conditions knows how dangerous it can be, especially at high speeds. Or, during the early morning hours, the rising summer sun will send its rays bouncing crazily off dirty windshields. By then the drivers are tired. Seeing through the tricky glare is difficult.

One driver can't last through a whole day, particularly under those conditions. So the Le Mans regulations require driving teams. While one man is at the wheel, his partner will be dozing fitfully, trying to rest his strained eyes, or gulping down a quick cup of coffee. No driver is permitted to be behind the wheel more than a total of fourteen hours. And it would appear perfectly obvious that only a fool would try to make it all the way by himself.

But one man did try to go all the way on his own. In 1952 a Frenchman named Pierre Levegh decided to drive the Le Mans race all alone. At that time there was no rule against solo driving, probably because officials thought no one would be crazy enough to attempt it.

Levegh was a capable, experienced driver. The previous year, as co-driver of a Talbot, he and his partner had finished fourth in the great endurance classic. Even though he was well over fifty years of age, he would have been a welcome partner for almost any driver in the race. But to go the route alone—at his age—was almost certain suicide. No one could talk him out of it. Levegh had made his decision and stuck to it. He believed—and many experts agreed—that his Talbot was the fastest entry and probably the strongest. If any car would finish, it was the Talbot. And Levegh was convinced he could finish too.

From the start of the race, through the late afternoon and into the night Levegh maintained perfect control of his car. If he felt weariness, he managed to shake it off, keeping to his planned pace. Other cars dropped out but Levegh drove on. By morning he was leading by four laps and there were only a few cars left to challenge him.

As the day wore on and Levegh held on to his lead the crowd began to sense history in the making. One man's name was on everyone's lips—Levegh. It seemed wildly impossible that a middle-aged man could fight off fatigue, keep his mind alert over the twenty-four hour grind, and beat off the other, younger drivers. But he was doing it!

Bleary-eyed, Levegh tooled the Talbot into the race's final hour, still ahead by some twenty-five miles. His brain had lost its sharpness long ago, and the game Frenchman was driving on sheer instinct, making the necessary split-second decisions as if in a dream. As the minutes ticked on his reflexes were even more dulled, his vision hazy, his eyelids heavy.

Finally, going into a curve, instead of shifting into a higher gear, he shifted down. The Talbot's engine sputtered and conked out.

Sick at heart, sick in body, Levegh was taken off the track weeping. Later, Le Mans officials decided that he had been more foolhardy than brave and decreed that no driver would be permitted to drive the day-long course alone.

Levegh continued to race at Le Mans. In 1955 he was co-driver of a Mercedes. A couple of hours after the race began, an Austin-Healy, driven by Lance Macklin, swerved and spun out in order to avoid a collision. Right behind Macklin was Levegh, roaring along at 150 miles an hour. He had no chance to clear Macklin's car. The Mercedes practically climbed up and over the Austin-Healy. Levegh's car flipped upside down and crashed into a crowd clustered near an embankment. The car exploded, killing Levegh and eighty-three spectators. It was by far the worst tragedy in the history of Le Mans.

There have been many spectacular crashes at Le Mans, as there have been at all races. Thankfully, most of the time the drivers have escaped death or serious injury. The loss in terms of money is always high. These sports cars are extremely expensive, costing as much as $80,000 each, and quite often more than that. Shipping the cars to Le Mans; hiring drivers and pit crews; providing spare parts, tires, and engines; purchasing high-octane fuel and special lubricants; can cost an automobile manufacturer almost a million dollars for that single race. Considering that first prize money amounts to about $16,000, a newcomer to racing might wonder why a manufacturer would spend a fortune when the cash return is so small.

The best reason is prestige. When a car wins, or makes a good showing at Le Mans, sports car buyers know that it has passed the most demanding test. They will buy a production model of that car as soon as it rolls off the assembly line. One year the Ford Mustang performed well in the race and the sale of Mustangs soared, in America, France, and other countries.

For Enzo Ferrari, manufacturer of fine Ferrari cars, sports car racing was always a combination of hobby and business investment. After his son died of leukemia at the age of twenty-four, Ferrari devoted himself to racing constantly. It was the only way he could forget, even momentarily, his deep sorrow.

For many years the Ferraris dominated at Le Mans. From 1958 through 1965 the Ferraris won seven of eight races, the last six in succession. Even when Ford began entering the endurance race the Ferraris continued to sweep the field. Finally, in 1966, the Ford entries finished 1–2–3, while no Ferraris were left on the course when the race ended. *Il Commendatore*—The Commander, as Ferrari was called—determined to avenge his defeat the following year.

For the 1967 race Ferrari's designers produced a new prototype car, powered by a twelve-cyclinder 450 horsepower engine. It wasn't the most powerful engine Ferrari could have used; in fact even some of his regular production cars had more powerful engines. But the "P-4," as Ferrari called the entry, weighed only 1,875 pounds and the engine had all the juice the frame could handle. The P-4 could brake more quickly and handle more easily.

Ford responded with the Mark IV, a 2,205 pound, 500

horsepower beauty, practically the same machine that had won at Sebring a few months earlier. On a straight-away it was faster than the Ferrari, but there weren't that many straight sections on the course. It was slightly more difficult to brake the Ford and somewhat harder to handle the wheel. Yet none of these factors meant as much as endurance. The basic question was, could the Ford outlast the Ferrari?

Of course other manufacturers entered the race, but somehow the experts felt that it would be a two-car contest, that the Porsches, Alpine-Renaults, Chaparrals, and others were there merely to fill out the number of cars required to make a respectable showing.

The great drivers were there too, including Mario Andretti, Roger McCluskey, Bruce McLaren, Chris Amon, and Ludovico Scarfiotti. Among the younger, up-and-coming drivers were Mark Donohue and Dan Gurney. And all of them looked with great respect at one of the Ford drivers, A. J. Foyt, fresh from a great victory in the Indianapolis 500.

For Anthony Joseph Foyt, Jr., racing came naturally. The son of a former racer, A. J. was driving miniature cars a few years after he learned to walk. Through his teen years Foyt raced just about anything with wheels, including motorcycles, stock cars, midgets, and sprint cars. Foyt was the youngest driver (he was just twenty-five years old then) in the 1958 Indianapolis race. The daring young Texan didn't win then; in fact he didn't even finish, spinning out on an oil slick just past the halfway mark. A. J. went all the way the following year, finishing tenth. He entered again in 1960 and once more was forced to drop out.

During those years Foyt entered other races and won many of them. Slowly he established himself as one of the best of the younger drivers. Finally, in 1961 he was first under the Indianapolis Speedway's checkered flag. He won out over the veteran Eddie Sachs by a scant eight seconds. Foyt was first again in 1964. And in 1967 he joined the select circle, which includes Wilbur Shaw, Mauri Rose, and Louis Meyer, to become one of the rare drivers to win the Indianapolis 500 three times.

Like so many other drivers, Foyt had rubbed shoulders with sudden death on several occasions. Once, in a stock car race at Riverside, California, Foyt went into a turn at 140 miles an hour when suddenly two cars in front of him slowed. Foyt tried to ease off too but his brakes failed. His car roared off the track and flew down an embankment end over end. Miraculously he escaped with broken bones and the loss of a good deal of skin. He could just as easily have been killed.

On another occasion a wheel snapped off his car while Foyt was zooming around at 150 miles an hour. The car skidded, bounced off a wall, and tore up the infield grass before lurching to a stop. Foyt walked away from that one, too.

But in spite of his unquestioned skill as a driver, A. J. had established his reputation on oval tracks. Le Mans is a tricky course, consisting of 8.36 miles of public roads. Even those drivers who have entered several times before have difficulty keeping a car under control lap after endless lap. Before the race every driver pores over detailed maps of the course, planning exactly how fast they will cover the ribbon of road known as Mulsanne Straight, how to move into the perilous Dunlop Bridge curve, how hard to brake through the various zigs and zags, the short crests and narrowings in the road.

Foyt was starting from scratch; the whole course was a mystery to him. Another handicap was his co-driver, Dan Gurney.

Although he was one of the best young drivers in the

business, Gurney had the reputation of being a "hard luck guy." The son of a former opera singer, Gurney's great interest in life was driving anything with wheels. He had driven old stock cars, go-karts, cycles, sports cars, and formula cars of all numbers, winning often enough to be respected by the wisest veterans. But he also lost many races through plain misfortune. On one occasion his steering wheel broke, and that practically never happens to anyone in a race. Gurney almost won the twelve-hour Sebring one year. He was well ahead on the last lap when his engine quit without warning. Only a short time before the Le Mans race he had been running strongly in the Indianapolis 500, but again was forced out with a broken piston. A fouled fuel line took him out of the Belgian Grand Prix.

The Le Mans start is different from the usual wave of a starter's flag. At four o'clock drivers line up on one side of the road while their cars are on the other side. When the signal is given the drivers race to their cars, hop in, and the event begins with a roar of engines and squealing of tires.

By five o'clock, an hour after the race had begun, the Fords were 1–2–3. Dan Gurney, driving a flame-red car, was well into the lead. Soon he pulled in, leaped out, and was replaced behind the wheel by Foyt. At ten o'clock the Foyt-Gurney team was four laps ahead, but now a Ferrari was in second place. The blue number-four Ford, driven by the team of Denis Hulme and Lloyd Ruby, developed mechanical trouble. Late that night another Ford was forced to drop out.

Ferraris were also running into all sorts of difficulties. Chris Amon's tire went flat and he was unable to change it because no one had remembered to put a flashlight in the car. Trying to drive to the pit, Amon was startled to see the tire catch fire. The flames spread to the car itself and Amon hopped out with only seconds to spare. Later, another Ferrari developed fuel injection trouble.

Even the best drivers could suddenly lose control of their cars on that course. It happened to Mario Andretti. He took the Dunlop Bridge curve flat out and didn't quite get all the way through. The car spun, caromed between two walls, and came to a dead stop in the middle of the road. Along came Roger McCluskey zooming into the same curve, and there was Andretti's car in his path. McCluskey had no choice but to scrape the wall too, and he bounced around until the car came to a stop. Seconds later another Ford arrived, tried to steer through but couldn't quite make it, and the pile-up was increased by one more car. The three drivers suffered only minor injuries, but as another driver said later, "It was terrible. There were pieces of cars all over the road."

Through the night more cars fell out. Gunter Klaus went into a spin, bounced into the trees, and his car broke apart. Mike Salmon's entry caught fire. The others went around and around, with Foyt and Gurney clinging grimly to their lead, hotly pursued by three Ferraris.

Dawn broke. The tired drivers, their every muscle stiff and sore, continued to spell each other. The Ford still led, but the Ferrari driven by Ludovico Scarfiotti began to cut the margin. Scarfiotti might have moved even closer, but now there were series of oil slicks covering several long stretches of the road. A faster pace would have to wait until the sun was high enough to dry off some of the slicker spots.

By eleven o'clock in the morning, with five hours still to go, thirty-nine cars had dropped out of the race. Only sixteen were left, including two Fords and two Ferraris. And they rolled on, as Mike Parkes relieved Scarfiotti and

Dan Gurney relieved Foyt. The early morning crowd saw the Ferrari gain ground, cutting the Ford's lead from seven laps to four.

Each time the Ferrari passed the Ford, to erase another lap from the lead, Foyt or Gurney would hold steady. They refused to panic, but stuck to the plans they had made before and during the race. They realized that the Mark IV would stand up and it was only a question of hanging on, refusing to take unnecessary chances. Time was on their side.

The hands of the clock spun and the exhausted drivers continued on. For the Ferrari it now seemed hopeless. Somehow, Scarfiotti could not cut into the four-lap lead any longer. It was a lost cause. But losing drivers don't quit just because they are behind. Anything can happen in a race, and it was always possible for the Ford to break down.

That didn't happen. Foyt was driving during the final lap, and he eased off the throttle slightly to insure final victory. Almost ready to fall asleep behind the wheel, A. J. Foyt drove through the checkered flag, blinking his lights, then slowing down momentarily so that the elated Dan Gurney could hop on the hood for the joyful winners' ride.

In second place, thirty-two miles behind, was the Ferrari driven by the gallant team of Ludovico Scarfiotti and Mike Parkes.

All sorts of records were broken. The winning Ford had covered 388 laps and averaged 135.482 miles per hour, 10 miles an hour faster than the previous record. In total, Foyt-Gurney had driven 3,220 miles!

But Ford, Foyt, and Gurney had yet another reason to celebrate. It was the first time an American car, driven by American drivers, had ever won at Le Mans!

## NURBURGRING

In the mid-1920s many German workers were unemployed. To provide them with jobs, government officials hit upon the idea of building a new race course. It would be a large one so that as many workers as possible would have an income. A site was selected just outside the tiny village of Nurburg, located in the Eifel Mountains, which lie along the western edge of Germany, between the Rhine River and Belgium. It had always been a tourist area, and the officials reasoned that racing fans would also like to view the ruins of an ancient twelfth century castle high on a hill.

The result of all the work and planning turned out to be one of the most fiendishly difficult courses in the world of racing. "The Ring," as it is popularly called, is slightly more than fourteen miles long. It wanders up and down hills, through pine forests, over public and connecting roads. There are numerous "bumps"—little rises in the road—so that sometimes, when going over a small crest at high speed, the car literally hangs in the air momentarily, all four wheels off the ground! Suspensions absorb a terrific beating.

Everywhere there are terrifying curves and corners, more than 170 in a lap. Some are switchbacks; the car is going in one direction and, after negotiating the turn, is moving in almost exactly the opposite direction.

Of all the turns at Nurburgring, the toughest, trickiest of all is called "The Karussel" (or Carousel). And in a way it certainly is like a merry-go-round as the name suggests. A car comes hurtling up a steep grade about 140 miles an hour, goes around a blind corner, and is confronted by something that looks like a large semi-circular cereal bowl, with the sides of the bowl tilted about thirty degrees. Driver Jackie Stewart once wrote that it reminded him of a "motorcycle wall of death." The road seems to fall away from under the wheels. The driver shifts down quickly into second gear and hangs on for dear life. On the Karussel a car's suspension is tested to the limit. Going into the turn, it sways in one direction; coming out of the turn it sways in the opposite direction. If the car comes out of the turn too high it could result in a skid; or even worse, it can leave the road and plow on into the woods.

Then there is the Adenau Descent, a three-quarter mile downhill section that ends at the Adenau Bridge. The descent begins with a left turn around a hedge, taken at high speed. That in itself isn't so bad, but it's followed by three successive right-hand turns. Therefore, to give himself room, an experienced driver will make the left turn on the outside, with his wheels brushing the edge of the hedge. But he doesn't dare cut it too fine, because beyond the hedge is a long drop into the valley. Then come those right turns, followed by more left turns and finally over the bridge. Drivers usually move down the twisting road pretty fast because it's a good spot to make up lost time. It is also a good spot to meet death.

Drivers study and re-study the course constantly, but it doesn't help much. No one can remember every wriggle, every crest and shallow as the road goes up and down. So they try to memorize the roughest curves and in that they are fairly successful. Some drivers, who have traveled the course many times, claim that they think one or two turns ahead. As they move from one hairpin they are already setting up their moves for the next one and the next.

But even planning ahead sometimes doesn't help. There is little a driver can do once he shoots around a blind turn and is suddenly confronted by a stalled car. He grips the wheel and tries to avoid the collision—if he can.

Then there is the weather to contend with. Sunshine can swiftly turn to rain, or fog, or hail, or even snow. All the pre-planning means nothing. The driver has to "play it by ear" as he water-skis through puddles and spins over oil slicks.

The roads themselves aren't always in top shape either. Why? Because racing is like any other sport. It is a business, admissions must be charged if a track is to make money. And in that respect Nurburgring is at a disadvantage.

Every year many thousands of people come to the Ring area on a camping weekend. They string out everywhere through the forest. It's impossible to tell who is a paying customer and who isn't. The course is much too long to police it constantly.

To make up for their losses, Nurburgring officials encourage the general public to take a lap around the course—after the race, of course. It costs less than a dollar per car. Some visitors hire an old-time race driver to come along with them, and the knowledgeable veterans will tell the history of the course as it is covered: over there a Mercedes went through the hedges and the driver was killed . . . on that curve somebody hit a tree . . . a bad pile-up on this spot a few years ago. But the trouble starts when some "civilians" try to act like race drivers. A few minutes after the course has been opened to the public, the calls go out for the fire trucks, the wreckers, and the ambulances; as cars go off the road, into hedges, into fences, into trees, and into each other. As a result there are bumps in the road that weren't planned by the Nurburgring builders. Since it would be extremely expensive to resurface the roads constantly, race drivers are always afraid they'll run into bumps that weren't there the year before.

Many tracks see a lot of use during racing season and

the Ring is no exception. When the European Grand Prix is held in Germany, Nurburgring is the scene. The same goes for the German Grand Prix. There are also various sports car races and all kinds of large and small Formula events, some even on Grand Prix day.

By far the toughest, most grueling car-killer of all the races is the Nurburgring 1000—forty-four laps of sheer torture. It is a sports car race with various types of entries, some more powerful than others. Regardless of the notable drivers and the magnificent cars, the real star of this race is the course itself. The drivers know it, so do the manufacturers of motor cars.

The first Ring 1000 was held in 1953 and was won by a Ferrari driven by two immortals, Albert Ascari and Giuseppe Farina. They finished with an average speed of 74.75 miles per hour. The fastest time during the early years was 84.26 mph, set in 1958 by Stirling Moss and Jack Brabham, sharing an Aston-Martin. For years three cars dominated the event: Ferrari, Aston-Martin, and Maserati. Other manufacturers never ceased trying to beat this fine trio of racing cars.

Eighty-four cars were on hand for the 1964 Nurburgring 1000. Ferrari was there as usual with a great lineup of cars. Jaguar entered four "E-type" models. There were a dozen Porsches, plus cars from Lotus Elan, MG, Alpine, Cobra, Aston-Martin, and others. For the first time Ford entered a GT at the Ring, to be driven by Phil Hill and Bruce McLaren. The Ford had fared badly at Le Mans a short time earlier and the rear part of the body had been modified so that it would hold the road better at high speeds.

The practice sessions that year were grim. During two of the three practice days the weather closed in with a foggy, wet grip, slicking the road dangerously. On Friday there were a dozen accidents, one of them fatal. Brian

Hetreed's Aston-Martin GT went off the road and into the trees as he was trying to change gears at 100 miles an hour. There was another shocker the next day. Rudolph Moser's Porsche went out of control. The car ran off the road, hit a ditch, and exploded, showering pieces of twisted wreckage on a parking lot a quarter of a mile away.

Yet, in spite of unfavorable weather conditions, records were set in the practice runs. Johnny Surtees ran off with top honors. In a 3.3 liter Ferrari, he turned in a lap in 8 minutes 57.9 seconds.

As 300,000 people strung out along the course, the race got under way with a Le Mans type start. Johnny Surtees broke into the lead and moved all alone into the South Curve. And he stayed there for a while. Surtees was clocked at 9 minutes and 9 seconds for his second lap; behind was Phil Hill in the Ford, followed by Graham Hill and Ludovico Scarfiotti in Ferraris. By the fifth lap Surtees had a fifty-second lead.

For some the race was over early. With the race barely under way, as the cars were jockeying for position, Bob Bondurant's Cobra banged into a Jaguar. Soon his tire went flat. He had no jack in the car, and it wouldn't have helped if he did. Bondurant rolled about twelve miles on that flat and finally reached the pit. There was no problem changing the wheel, but the bouncing had done some damage to the body. Bondurant went back into the race, only to pull in again later with a bad shock absorber. Again he went back but it was useless. Finally the Cobra's engine just quit.

Another Cobra became an also-ran when Jo Schlesser came in with a faulty alternator wire contact. By the time the trouble was traced and repaired, Schlesser was too far back to be considered a challenger.

More cars dropped out for numerous different reasons.

One car cracked up when it failed to come out of a hairpin turn. Another lost a wheel, spun crazily, and came to rest. A Jaguar continued to go around and around the course, but without much speed because it was stuck in third gear.

The Ford entrusted to Phil Hill and Bruce McLaren did not do well. Before the race was half over, it was out with a broken tie rod.

The Ferrari driven by Graham Hill and Innes Ireland was disqualified for illegal refueling. Ireland had run out of gas, sprinted to the pit and told what had happened. Officials reminded him that it was against the rules to refuel on the track, but Hill grabbed a can of gas and ran to the stalled Ferrari. As he started up and went by the officials' station, Hill was given the black flag—get off the road, you are disqualified. But they could have saved themselves the trouble. The reason the Ferrari had run out of fuel so unexpectedly soon became apparent. There were leaks all over the fuel tank and it couldn't have continued anyway.

Such incidents, and others, are all part of a race. The 1964 Nurburgring 1000 was no more and no less than a typical race between finely tuned machines and skilled drivers. Broken rods and leaking tanks and flat tires and stuck gearboxes and split wire contacts, all play a part in automobile racing.

Johnny Surtees clung to the lead, lost it briefly, and then after the second series of pit stops, was in front again. He and co-driver Lorenzo Bandini seemed to have the race all but sewed up. Chasing him, almost hopelessly, was the Ferrari driven by Ludovico Scarfiotti, the good-humored heir to a cement fortune; and his co-driver, Nino Vacarella, who had crashed in practice at Nurburgring the year before. Vacarella had been so badly injured that he could not enter another race for the rest of the year.

The 1000 was two-thirds over when Surtees suddenly lost a wheel and crashed. Shaken, disappointed, he climbed out of the damaged car and walked away.

Now the Scarfiotti/Vacarella Ferrari led, pursued by another Ferrari, driven by the team of Mike Parkes and Jean Guichet. And that was how it would end. It wasn't a fierce charge to the flag, with one car inches ahead of the other. Outside the movies, comparatively few races end that way.

Other drivers in other cars chased them to the end, going around and around the course fighting all sorts of difficulties. Jo Rindt, in another Ferrari, had been going well in spite of his car's handicaps. That particular Ferrari was uncomfortable and tough to drive. The noise, the gas fumes, and the pounding he took made Rindt sick at one point and he came into the pit for relief. But his co-driver had taken off for a quick shower. So Rindt, his insides heaving, went through another lap.

So ended another Nurburgring 1000, 623.5 miles of torture for both man and car. The average of 87 miles per hour was a new record. It would be broken.

In one way it was a victory for Ferrari. His cars had finished first, second, fourth, and seventh. But the other six cars finishing among the first ten were manufactured by Porsche, so it was a Porsche victory too.

After it was over, American manufacturers sadly noted that European car makers still had the Nurburgring 1000 locked up. In time that too would change.

## TARGA FLORIO

Usually, a race is named after a geographical location. The Grand Prix races have "nationalities," such as Monaco, Dutch, Belgian, German, and so on. The noted sports car races are named for regional sites, such as Le Mans in France, Sebring and Daytona in Florida, and the rest.

The Targa Florio is named after a man.

A Sicilian noble, Count Vincenzo Florio, was one of the earliest racing fans. Back in 1904 he donated a cup for the winner of a race held in Brescia, Italy. Later, he decided that what was good enough for Italy was also good enough for his beloved Sicily. He promoted a new race, which was first held in 1906. The course was laid out all around that Mediterranean island, and led through some of the roughest mountain roads ever climbed by any automobile.

The first race, over what was then a ninety-mile course, was won by Alessandro Cagno driving an Itala. Even considering the fact that cars of that era went at a comparative snail's pace, Cagno's time was slow. He averaged 29.07 miles per hour for the 277.3 mile race. But in all fairness, nobody could have gone very fast through those wilderness roads, and in modern times the speed of a winning car hasn't increased too much. Actually, the Targa Florio is the slowest of all the sports car races.

That first race was not without humor. Cagno was delirious with joy at his victory. As he crossed the finish line he slammed down on the brakes so hard that he broke the car!

The date of that first race, May 6, 1906, makes this Sicilian event the oldest such race of all. About fifty days later, the Automobile Club of France instituted the first Grand Prix at Le Mans.

The old course has been shortened and now it covers about forty-four miles or so, but it is still one of the most rugged to be found in any country. A witty spectator once described the course as "part hillclimb and part road race; and all the entries are part cars, part mountain goats." The road winds into the Madonie Mountains, twisting and turning like a tangle of snakes thrown onto the ground. For any car, regardless of its power, second gear is the most important. Third gear is seldom used, and fourth gear is employed primarily on the long straight running along the seaside. Therefore, it can be said that a car moves on the average at about 60 miles an hour in second gear. That can play havoc with even the strongest gearbox.

There are stories told about a bandit who lived in the Madonie Mountains. He commanded an "army" of about a thousand men, and they preyed on all unwary travelers in the region. Even local farmers were sometimes his victims. But he never stopped a racing car because he enjoyed the Targa Florio immensely. Drivers told of seeing him sitting on a hilltop where he could watch the cars go by. They reported that he cheered them on. Eventually, the police caught up with him and the bandit was shot.

Although the drivers no longer look for the familiar figure of the bandit chief, they still have to be doubly wary of each other. Usually, more cars enter the Targa Florio than any other sports car race because manufacturers want the prestige of having their cars try to finish out the tough grind. Sometimes there are as many as eighty cars off the starting line, even though it is a foregone conclusion that only a few will be around at the end.

Because it is a traditional race—the oldest of all cross-country events—the big names in driving are there. In 1964, for instance, entries included Jo Bonnier, Graham Hill, Phil Hill, Bob Bondurant, Dan Gurney, and Innes Ireland. But many a lesser known driver was also there; their names were Grana, Coco, Davis, Pucci, Arena, and Tchotoua.

The cars took off from the starting line at thirty-second intervals under a bright morning sky. After one lap Jo Bonnier (teamed with Graham Hill) was in the lead in their 1963 eight-cylinder Porsche roadster. Edgar Barth in a Porsche 904 was second, and Dan Gurney, driving one of Carroll Shelby's 4.7 liter Cobras, was third. Bonnier's time for the first lap was 41 minutes 16.1 seconds, or slightly better than 60 miles per hour. In tenth spot was a part-time driver named Pucci, driving a production Porsche 904. The Sicilians among the spectators cheered him wildly, for Pucci lived in those parts.

During the second lap a few of the dropouts popped up. Actually, many fans were surprised that nobody had left in the first lap because that was usually the case. Ten cars were subtracted, including Bonnier's Porsche. He radioed back to the pit from a signal depot at a hamlet called Bivio Polizzi that his rear U-joint was broken. In three cars the problem was a broken transmission. One car ran off the road, two had broken valves, and the rest had other assorted miseries. The jouncing, bouncing ride on those bad mountain roads proved anew that even the most carefully checked cars can break apart when conditions are bad.

Soon Dan Gurney's Cobra began to sputter because the car refused to stay in second gear and had to be held there. Another Porsche, handled by the team of Edgar Barth and Umberto Maglioli, broke a shock absorber and, by the time a new one was installed, they were out of it. More cars wheezed into the pits and the mechanics found broken chassis, jammed differentials, and that classic of all troubles, a broken wishbone.

The "wishbone" is a kind of A-shaped arm, part of the suspension system. When a car is driven over poor roads and is rattled around enough, this metal piece can break. It happened to Dan Gurney and Phil Hill, among others. Another Cobra, driven by Innes Ireland and Masten Gregory, first developed radiator trouble and then the throttle linkage came apart.

Perhaps, in a way, that is why manufacturers want their cars in the Targa Florio. For what is learned in a race like that is valuable. Production cars, coming off the assembly line, will be driven over poor roads. Manufacturers learn what can go wrong and try to correct the weak spots. Any trouble anyone could think of hit the cars in that forty-eighth Targa Florio. Suspension systems were a joke, valves and gears and throttle linkages and radiators and pistons and driveshafts and brakedrums and fan belts broke down, flew apart.

By the end of the sixth lap the Porsche driven by the Pucci/Davis team was out in front. As the car kept going Davis turned in a 41.09 lap, which was a record for cars in the 2-liter GT class. It also turned out to be the fastest lap by any car, regardless of its power, in that 1964 race.

Pucci/Davis finally won, covering the ten laps—447 miles—in 7 hours 10 minutes 53.3 seconds. Oddly, neither man had much of a reputation as an expert driver. In fact Pucci only entered one race a year usually, and that was the Targa Florio. His co-driver, Davis, occasionally drove in Junior races and the Targa Florio.

Two "part-time drivers" had won racing's oldest cross-country event!

# 4 · The Indianapolis 500

Every Memorial Day weekend the city of Indianapolis, Indiana, stages a spectacular festival. Many thousands of visitors from all over the United States and from other lands watch a huge parade, complete with marching bands, floats, and pretty girls. There is a teen-age fair and a $1,000 gin rummy tournament. The mayor invites visiting officials from other cities to a special breakfast. Later there are special banquets and a Governor's Ball. Normally Indianapolis is an average, quiet city, but for this event it becomes a gigantic open-air carnival.

The main attraction, the event the crowds have really come to see, is an automobile race around an oval track. Enthusiastic fans declare firmly that it is the greatest, most important of all races, that no other event can compare. They refer to it as "Indy" or just "the 500." The full name of this exhausting, nerve-racking race is *The Indianapolis 500*.

It isn't a sports car race because the cars have open cockpits, are single-seaters, and are by no means production models. Nor is it a Formula race because the cars do not have the same engine restrictions. The Indianapolis 500 is in a class by itself.

On the eve of the race, cars, trucks, and campers line up outside the Speedway. At dawn aerial bombs explode and the track opens for business. What follows resembles a cattle stampede as 75,000 vehicles storm through the gates into the infield, jockeying around for the most advantageous positions. Finally they all settle down, and for the rest of the day the infield is like a monster cookout-picnic, as barbecues are started, sandwiches and coffee and soda pop and beer are consumed.

Meanwhile, more fans stream into the stands. Considering that general admission costs $5, seats in the backstretch bleachers cost $10, and the covered penthouse seats on the main straightaway cost $40, the track's box office reaps a gigantic harvest of money. In addition, television will pay a tidy sum for permission to show the race on home screens. About 300,000 fans will view the race in person, but many millions will watch it on television.

The Indianapolis 500 had always been popular with racing fans, but for a time the future of the track looked doubtful. Before World War II it was owned by a group of people headed by former flying ace Captain Eddie Rickenbacker. They did little to maintain the condition of the stands or other facilities. During the war, no races were held and the track began to go to seed. After the war it was purchased by Anton Hulman, Jr. After the very first race he realized how much work was needed to make the historic Speedway a first class track. Everything was falling apart. In fact a few fans actually did fall through the rotting wood planks of the stands.

Hulman spent millions making improvements, putting all the track's profits into modernizing the Speedway. Now the bleachers are concrete and steel, and all the timing devices are the newest electronic types.

Practically every notable driver in the world is eager to get behind the wheel of a car in the Indianapolis 500. The purses and prizes total slightly more than a million dollars, including about $200,000 in special prizes from manufacturers of various automotive equipment. At other tracks in America, the purses in a race sponsored by the United States Auto Club might total about $100,000 or perhaps a bit higher. Thus Indy offers ten times as much money and, it can also be said, ten times the glory.

It would be unfair to suggest that the 500 is ten times as tough as any other American race. But it is difficult enough for any car and driver.

First of all, a driver is faced with 200 laps at speeds varying up to 200 miles an hour on the straights.

Second, temperatures on the track surface rise to sickening, melting heights, as high as 145 degrees. Fumes from exhausts hang heavy as the cars zoom around the oval.

Third, those left turns—800 of them in the 200 laps—are much trickier than they look. Especially that first one. It takes time to learn how to handle it.

As the driver roars past the grandstand straightaway, there is some slight protection from the air currents. Then, as he leaves the shelter of the stands, he streaks into what can only be described as a "wind tunnel." While the driver fights the air currents, holding the wheel steady, he is faced with a slightly banked curve, the first turn. Many drivers find that they are forced to go deep into the turn, with the front end of the car pressing down and the rear end trying to rise up. It's like a wrestling match as the driver hangs on to the wheel, keeping the car on course. Jackie Stewart, certainly one of the best race drivers in the world, once wrote that he learned to take the turn following the methods of another great champion, Parnelli Jones. Parnelli (almost everyone refers to him by just his first name) eased off on the throttle and tapped the brakes about fifty yards earlier than Stewart. His car slowed, but it also stayed level while Stewart's was bumping along front and rear. As a result Parnelli could turn on the juice about 100 yards before Stewart was able to. When Stewart began following Parnelli's method, he increased his lap speed from 158 to 161 mph. At Indy or any other race that can mean a great deal.

The turns are only part of the track hazards. A driver must try to stay "in the groove." That is a kind of narrow lane around the track which most of the cars follow. Staying in the lane permits the driver to get the most speed from his car because he doesn't have to use the brakes as much. In other words it's really the shortest, fastest, safest "route" around the track. Of course a driver will leave the groove for many reasons, such as passing another car or avoiding a collision. In such cases he has to move inside the groove or outside it. But he had better get a good, fresh grip on the wheel. Jackie Stewart has described the track area outside the lane as "driving on ball bearings," because of the dust and grit that collects on the little-used portion of the track.

In many ways, knowing about the Indianapolis 500 is to receive an education in all of racing, including cars and drivers. It isn't that things happen at Indy first and then later at other tracks. In fact quite often it's the other way around. The "Brickyard" as Indy is often referred to is really a conservative track. Officials look with suspicion at radical changes. Sometimes the changes are adopted, sometimes they aren't. The cars themselves are an excellent example of how the great 500 mile race has changed, slowly but surely.

The cars racing at Indy right after World War II were "dirt track" vehicles. The engine was up front and the driver sat fairly high, in an almost upright position, almost directly over the driveshaft.

In the early 1950s the "roadster" design was introduced. Powered by an Offenhauser engine, the roadster was lower because the engine and drive train had been installed on the left side of the car. Soon almost all entries at Indy were roadsters, powered by "Offys" as the Offenhauser was affectionately called.

In 1961 Jack Brabham brought a Cooper-Climax to Indy. The engine was mounted in the rear. By comparison with the Offy roadsters, the Formula I type racer seemed to be a child's toy, and a funny-looking one at that. The Cooper-Climax couldn't compete with the roadsters in engine power. Brabham's car had a 168 cc engine, while the roadsters boasted 255 cc engines. On the straightaways the Cooper ate dust from the bigger cars. But Brabham went zooming around the turns like a scurrying beetle. And that year he finished ninth.

American officials merely shrugged their shoulders at Brabham. They thought he was just a "crazy foreigner" with crazy ideas. But Californian Dan Gurney thought the idea of a rear-engine car would work at Indy. In 1962 Gurney entered the 500 with a Mickey Thompson Special. It had been built in the United States. The car was powered by a Buick rear-mounted engine.

Gurney didn't win. In fact he didn't even finish the race. A broken rear end forced him out after ninety-two laps. Even so, Gurney was convinced that the future of Indy cars lay in rear-mounted engines. Furthermore, he knew just the man to design a winning car: Colin Chapman, the great British engineer, who had designed the Lotus Grand Prix cars. Gurney teamed Chapman with Ford engineers. The result was a 255 cc Lotus-Ford.

There were four rear-engine entries in the 1963 Indy race. Two were Lotus-Fords, one driven by Gurney, the other by the then up-and-coming Jim Clark. Mickey Thompson, encouraged by Gurney's good showing the previous year, also had two cars with rear-mounted Chevrolet engines.

The new-type cars were lower, lighter, more streamlined than the Offy roadsters. They also handled more easily, because each wheel had individual suspension, while the Offy roadsters had the old-fashioned solid axles.

The record book says that the 1963 Indianapolis 500 was won by Parnelli Jones in a conventional roadster. Jim Clark came in second, Dan Gurney came in seventh, and one of the Mickey Thompson cars finished ninth. But there are many experts who insist that Clark would have won if he had had more experience at the Indianapolis track. He wasn't used to the "hubcap-to-hubcap" competition, or those crazy turns. Besides, Parnelli's car was throwing oil toward the finish and every other driver still on the track was afraid of hitting a slick and going into a spin. One thing was perfectly clear: Jim Clark had the better car. Also, the front-engine car was on its way out.

Indeed, by 1965, when Jim Clark did win at Indianapolis—only four years after the rear-engine had been introduced—twenty-seven of the thirty-three qualifying cars in the race had engines mounted in the rear!

Just as USAC officials were getting used to rear engines, another radical new design shook them up. Andy Granatelli was the man who did the shaking.

Granatelli, a jovial, oversized mechanical genius, had worked his way up in the world. From a poverty-stricken childhood, he became a mechanic and driver, and finally president of the *STP Corporation*, a company which manufactures automotive products. Big Andy always loved to tinker with new ideas, new designs, new ways to make a car travel faster, safer, smoother. In 1967 he showed up at the Speedway with an entry called the STP Turbocar. This car had four-wheel drive. And it had a turbine engine, a Pratt and Whitney power plant that really belonged in a small airplane. The engine wasn't mounted in the front or rear; rather it was mounted *alongside* the driver, to his left.

Turbine engines (instead of the usual piston engines) had been tried at Indy before. So had four-wheel drive. And they had not been very successful. But the side-mounted engine was something else. Officials scratched their heads, as if they thought Granatelli were some kind of a nut.

In the practice runs, Parnelli Jones, who was Granatelli's driver, realized instantly that his boss wasn't nuts at all. The four-wheel drive gave the car fantastic traction. Parnelli didn't have to follow "the groove" at all, for he found he could take the turns in his own way and steer out of them beautifully. And that turbocar was FAST!

Wisely refusing to tip off what kind of whippet-fast car he was driving, Parnelli kept it in check and qualified for sixth position. Once the race started, it was obvious that Parnelli could have started thirty-third and still walked away from everybody.

Before the first lap was over, Parnelli had jumped into the lead. On the turns he followed his own course, clipping precious tenths-of-a-second off his normal time, and on the straights the turbine opened the gap still wider. The turbocar was like a flitting, zinging, maneuverable rabbit, outdistancing the slower, chasing hound dogs.

Bad weather halted the race after eighteen laps, but it was continued the following day. Parnelli took it easy, as if he were out for an afternoon of sight-seeing in the country. The turbocar passed the 490-mile mark with a comfortable lead. Then—goodbye! A transmission bearing broke and the turbocar slowed and rolled to a stop. A. J. Foyt in a Ford-Coyote went by to win.

USAC officials saw the handwriting on the wall. Granatelli had made the turbine work, and that might mean all the other cars would be obsolete. But there was too much at stake. Manufacturers had gigantic investments in piston engines. So new rules were introduced, aimed at stopping turbines.

*Veteran driver Graham Hill, who always gave a good account of himself in every race that he entered.*

*Monaco: Jim Clark in his Lotus trying very hard at Gasworks Hairpin about halfway through the race.*

*The great Jim Clark.*

FIRESTONE TIRE & RUBBER COMPANY, INC.

*Teacher and pupil: Jack Brabham (left) and Denis Hulme. In 1967, they battled it out to the finish in the Mexican Grand Prix.*

GOODYEAR TIRE & RUBBER COMPANY

*The Ford Mark IV, which won at Se-*
*bring and Le Mans in 1967.*

STP CORPORATION

FIRESTONE TIRE & RUBBER COMPANY, INC.

*Only fourteen years apart, the progress in racing car design is obvious: note the difference in the wider tires, the low-slung chassis, the difference in the suspension system.*

*Mario Andretti finally gets winning checker at Indianapolis driving "back-up" STP-Hawk.*

A. J. Foyt after his third Indianapolis victory in 1967. Right after that he won at Le Mans.

Famous sons of famous fathers: Bill Vukovich Jr. and Gary Bettenhausen.

*Denis Hulme tests the new Gulf-McLaren M20.*

*Bruce McLaren, who was the great designer of the cars that won the Can-Am in 1970.*

Turbine engines depend on air intake—great gobs of air. If the air intake is reduced, the engine does not work as well. So USAC rules reduced the air intake from 23.999 square inches to 15.999 inches.

Granatelli raged and screamed and took his case to court. He lost. Undaunted, he complied with the new regulations, and in 1968 Granatelli returned to Indy with three new turbocars. Unfortunately, it was a case of history almost repeating itself. With a little more than twenty-two miles to go, a Granatelli car, driven by Joe Leonard, was in the lead. But it was forced out with a broken fuel pump.

Again the USAC clamped down on turbocars, further reducing the air intake to 11.999 square inches. Nobody could figure out a way to design a turbine engine that would meet those specifications.

But there is another aspect of the great Indianapolis 500, and it has nothing to do with USAC officials, or manufacturers, or square inches of air intake. It concerns the drivers. For them this Memorial Day race is the most important event of all. To win it is the dream of every man who ever gripped a wheel.

They begin thinking seriously about the race in spring. Their households are filled with talk about the upcoming Indy 500. They talk of the prize money and the glory. And the young boys—the drivers' sons and kid brothers—listen, entranced. Almost all these youngsters also begin to dream about the time when *they* will become race drivers and enter the Indianapolis 500. And it does happen, as the 1968 race shows. But first it is necessary to go back a few years in order to describe the men in whose footsteps the youngsters followed.

No driver in history was more daring, more reckless than Bill Vukovich. Born in California, raised on a farm, "Vukie" began racing when he was barely eighteen years old. He started with stock cars and progressed into midget racers. So did his brother, Eli. But Bill was clearly the superior driver, winning the West Coast Midget Championship in 1946 and 1947, and the National Midget Championship in 1950. After that he was ready for bigger, more important races.

By then his recklessness had earned for him the nickname "The Mad Russian." He took chances no other driver would think of attempting.

Still Vukovich was smart enough to know when he had a chance to win a race and when it was hopeless. In 1951, his first entry in the Indy 500, Vukovich drove a car called the *Central Excavating Special.* Even after he had qualified in it, Vukovich declared that he didn't think the car would hold together for thirty laps. He was almost right; the car made only twenty-nine laps.

The following year, 1952, Vukie was back in a better car. He was more confident of winning. And he might have, but for mechanical trouble. He was leading by about half a lap with 100 miles to go when the steering began to act up. Vukie kept on, fighting the wheel, clinging precariously to a narrowing lead. Finally, with twenty-five miles to go and still leading by half a mile, the pivot pin on the steering column broke. Vukie slid along, scraping the wall. The car stopped. Troy Ruttman, at the age of twenty-two the youngest to win at Indy, swept by to win.

It was then, while he was sitting on the wall and watching the cars go by, that Vukovich uttered the immortal words, "It's not hard to win here. All you've got to do is keep turning left."

Vukovich returned to Indianapolis in 1953, more determined than ever. It was a brutally hot day and many drivers were anxious to be relieved during the race. Only a handful went all the way without relief. One of them, Carl Scarborough, later died of heat exhaustion. Vukovich was one of the few who drove through the entire race, pushing himself and the car beyond all reasonable limits. He ignored the stifling heat and the fumes that hung over the track like a smothering blanket. Vukie led by about three laps at the halfway mark, and took the checkered flag eight miles ahead of his nearest rival.

And in 1954 Bill Vukovich made it back-to-back victories at Indianpolis. He simply outlasted the others, leading for the final 125 miles and coming in about a lap and a half ahead of a driver named Jimmy Bryan.

In 1955 Bill Vukovich was on hand at Indy again, trying for his third straight 500 victory. Other drivers had won the 500 three times in the past: Louis Meyer, Wilbur Shaw, and Mauri Rose; in years to come A. J. Foyt would also be a three-time winner. But nobody had ever won three times in succession.

Vukie started out in fifth position, but soon was leading the pack. After the first fifty-six laps (Vukovich had been in the lead for fifty of them) he closed in on the last-place cars, ready to begin lapping the field.

Suddenly, a grim pile-up loomed ahead. Rodger Ward's axle broke and he swerved out of control. Al Keller had to move swiftly to avoid the careening car and he sideswiped Johnny Boyd's car. Right behind them was Vukovich. And the man who had said "always turn left" was forced to turn to the right.

It was practically a broadside collision. Vukovich's left front wheel hit Boyd's right rear wheel, shearing it off. Vukovich and his car flew high, crashed, went end-over-end, and burst into flames. The great, reckless "Mad Russian" was dead.

Bill Vukovich wasn't a popular champion, at least with the other drivers. He wasn't a backslapper and he didn't like to take part in victory parties. After a race Vukie usually packed his bags and went home to California to be with his family. But there was one driver he liked, a friendly, grinning chap. His name was Melvin Eugene Bettenhausen, but everyone called him Tony.

Like Vukovich, Tony Bettenhausen was raised on a farm. After his father died the Bettenhausen farm was sold, but later Tony bought it back.

How Tony Bettenhausen survived as long as he did was something of a mystery. Tough Tony earned two nicknames. One was "Flip," the other was "Cementhead." Both nicknames were for the same reason. During various races he had flipped upside down twenty-eight times by his own count. And always he had come out of the crack-up to race another day.

Bettenhausen won the United States driving championship twice, in 1951 and 1958. A few other times he came close. During his 1951 championship season, he won a number of 100-mile races: at Langhorne Speedway in Pennsylvania, at Milwaukee, at Springfield, and at Du Quoin, Illinois. But oddly enough, in 1958 he didn't win any championship races. However, he usually placed high enough to pile up points and that was how he won the championship a second time. That only proved Tony Bettenhausen was one of the most consistently good drivers of his time. Yet he never did win at Indianapolis.

In 1955 Tony Bettenhausen achieved his highest Indy finish, coming in second. And he kept trying, convinced that some day the great 500-mile race would be his. He entered fourteen times. The 1961 race was to be his fifteenth.

One of Bettenhausen's old friends, Paul Russo, was having some trouble with his car but couldn't put his finger on what was wrong. He asked Bettenhausen to check it out during practice. Friendly, always eager to help, Tony Bettenhausen did—and it cost him his life. He had the car traveling flat out when it began to sway. A cotter pin—a little piece of metal that costs a nickel or a dime—hadn't been put in properly. It fell out. The car smashed through and over the wall, ripping down posts and wires as it kept flipping over. It was Tony Bettenhausen's final flip.

But the names Vukovich and Bettenhausen were not meant to die out at the Indianapolis Speedway. The race had become almost a part of the families of both men. And so, two drivers bearing those names qualified for the 1968 race: Gary Bettenhausen and Billy Vukovich Jr., sons of the two outstanding drivers.

But they weren't the only members of the large "Indy family of drivers." In 1958, just ten years earlier, a fine driver named Jerry Unser, who had come from a racing family, survived a bad crash at the Speedway. Only the year before that, Jerry had been USAC stock car champion. In 1959, a year after he had survived the crack-up, Jerry Unser was killed while practicing at Indianapolis.

The Unser name was destined to come back into the lists of Indianapolis entries. In 1968 two more Unsers were entered at Indy: Jerry's brothers, Bobby and Al. Bobby, driving an Eagle-Turbo-Offy, was in third position. Al, in a Lola-Turbo-Ford, was in sixth spot. First and second positions had been won by Joe Leonard and Graham Hill, driving the Andy Granatelli cars.

The field broke away cleanly with Leonard leading. But, as was mentioned earlier, it was not to be his day, nor Andy Granatelli's. At the eighth lap Bobby Unser grabbed first place and began a duel with Leonard.

It happens quite often in a race that one accident knocks out several cars. That's what happened on the forty-first lap. Al Unser lost a right front wheel and smacked into the wall at the first turn. He wasn't hurt, but pieces of wreckage hit the cars driven by Arnie Knepper and Gary Bettenhausen.

For a while the race settled down into a hassle between Bobby Unser, Joe Leonard, and Lloyd Ruby, the latter driving a Mongoose-Turbo-Offy. Less than four seconds separated the trio. And, after 350 miles, they were still fighting it out as the gap between them got even narrower. It was the same story; on the turns, Leonard's lighter, more maneuverable STP car beat the piston engines, but on the 3,300-foot straightaways, Leonard just didn't have the speed.

By the three-quarter mark it was Unser by a heartbeat, Ruby second, Leonard third, and Dan Gurney, in an Eagle-Gurney-Ford in fourth spot. Unser's car was not going at peak speed because he had been stuck in fourth gear for some time. When he left the pits with a full load of fuel he had to "slip the clutch" in order to pick up speed.

Then Ruby began to sputter as his ignition coil went bad. It would have been his race but for that. It took 6 minutes and 29 seconds to make the repair, and by the time he got going again the others were long gone.

So Leonard led until the 191st lap, when his transmission conked out. And Bobby Unser, hanging in there, drove to victory, with Dan Gurney second, and Mel Kenyon third.

Billy Vukovich came in seventh. That was also the year he won Rookie-of-the-Year honors. As for Gary Bettenhausen, he had merely run into bad luck because of someone else's mishap.

There is one added note to this story about drivers of the same family competing at Indianapolis. In 1970 it was the turn of Bobby's brother, Al Unser, to win the 500. It was the first time brothers had ever won the Indianapolis 500.

It has been said that a race driver's family is as much a part of racing as he is, especially the young boys—the sons or brothers of the driver. The lucky drivers hang around for years. Therefore, it is quite possible that some

day, when the cry is raised at the Indianapolis Speedway
—"Gentlemen, start your engines!"—that somewhere
among the entries there may be a father competing
against his son!

# 5 · The Can-Am Series

Grand Prix cars have limitations imposed on engine capacity. In one sense that is what the word "formula" means. Although the limits are changed from time to time, depending on the formula of a particular type of car, still there are restrictions.

Sports cars also have some limitations. Sometimes only certain modifications are permitted on production cars. And manufacturers must produce a certain number of cars of each type during a production year.

Years ago racing fans, engineers, and drivers began to dream of the "fastest" cars, the most powerful cars, racing machines with no limits. They pictured big booming engines, mounted on specially designed frames, with sleek, tough chassis boring through the wind. And they wondered how fast such cars could go, especially in the hands of the greatest drivers.

The dream has come true in today's *Group 7* cars.

According to Appendix J of the International Sporting Code of the FIA, Group 7 has no limitation on engine power, body weight, or the size of wheels and tires. It is true that the regulations insist on certain features: the car must be a two-seater, run on pump gas, and have a self starter. Each car must be equipped with a dual brake system run by the same foot pedal. If one system fails, the backup brake system goes into operation automatically.

Otherwise, designers are free to do anything they like.

The outstanding drivers of long ago, such as Louis Chiron, Rex Mays, Mauri Rose, and the rest would have been bewildered by the design, the power, and the performance of these sleek monsters. For, once restrictions were lifted, the great designers of cars such as Bruce McLaren, Jim Hall, and the others had a chance to put all their theories to the test. The results have been amazing.

Imagine a car that can spurt up to more than 100 miles an hour in low gear! Imagine a car that can zoom away with tires squealing, reach the 100-mph mark, and then come to a dead stop, all in ten seconds! Quite simply, a Group 7 car is the fastest racer on any track, in any race.

The two important words are "track" and "race." For it is also true that the cars running the Bonneville Salt Flats are far faster. But those cars don't go around a track. They just take off over a measured distance, running straight ahead on the dry lake bed. There is no way these jet-powered jobs can take a hairpin turn. Streaking along at more than 400 miles an hour, they would just sail away from the track like an airplane taking off. And these experimental cars don't race each other anyway. They are running against the clock.

A Group 7 car is usually referred to as a *sports-racing* car. The hyphen between the words sports and racing is important (sometimes a slant sign [/] is used) because it distinguishes Group 7 from Group 5 cars. The latter, also very fast and powerful, have some restrictions.

Most drivers and car designers are certain that a Group 7 car can reach a top speed of 250 miles an hour. They have not been pushed that fast because no track has a straightaway long enough to allow the driver to jam down on the throttle and go flat out. But it is known that a Le Mans Ford Mark IV can do about 220 miles an hour. A top Group 7 car, which might have 100 horse-power more than a Mark IV, figures to be faster.

While all Group 7 cars have the usual differences in design, many of them have one thing in common. In a way, the designers went back to the old ways of design; the engines are powerful but the chassis and frames are lightweight. In the old days that was dangerous. Today, with new, improved, modern alloys, designers have all the body strength they need.

The chassis of a Group 7 car is usually made of an alloy of aluminum and magnesium, or titanium, or any other light but strong metal. The body shell can be made of tough fiber glass. The engine block may be aluminum. There is a fuel injection system. And oddly, while many of the designs may be European, the engines are Ameri-can. Very often they are built by Chevrolet.

Group 7 cars sometimes race in European hillclimbs, and occasionally they run in Japan. But mostly, they are seen regularly in Canada and the United States in a series of races called The Canadian-American Challenge Cup, or, as it is more popularly called, the *Can-Am.*

The Can-Am of the 1970s consists of ten or eleven races and is staged at various North American tracks. The prizes for these events total more than a million dollars in purses and other awards. But the drivers know that it isn't really a great test of skill. All races need topnotch drivers, but in the Can-Am series, the man behind the wheel of the best car will win. And it was in the Can-Am that Bruce McLaren came into his own as a designer of racing cars.

In 1966, when the Can-Am began, Johnny Surtees was the hero of the series. There were only six races in the Can-Am then and Surtees won three of them, driving a Lola Type 70 with a Chevrolet engine. But after that the Can-Am became almost the private property of McLaren.

With the help of designer Robin Herd, McLaren and his team won with monotonous regularity. The New Zealander drove one of the cars and several skilled drivers handled the others. If McLaren was the number-one man, then the number-two driver of Team McLaren was fellow New Zealander, Denis Hulme.

Denny's father, Clive Hulme, was a World War II hero; he won the Victoria Cross, the British Empire's highest award. After the war he returned to New Zealand and opened a garage. Denny entered his father's business after he finished school, and it was tinkering with cars in the garage that sparked his interest in racing.

Young Hulme drove all sorts of vehicles, including 2-liter Coopers. In 1960 he followed in Bruce McLaren's footsteps, going to Europe on the "racing scholarship." He did all right, too, winning the Formula II section of the International Trophy at Silverstone, England. Later, he entered a few races on the continent.

Hulme's career continued to follow McLaren's when he too hooked up with Jack Brabham. Hulme became a sort of combination mechanic–driver–builder's-helper, and he learned plenty from the great three-time champion. In 1963 Hulme really established himself as a driver with a brilliant future. In fourteen races of various kinds he won seven and finished second four times. And he found himself in excellent company for, as the years passed, Brabham assembled a great team, including McLaren, Hulme, and Dan Gurney.

Careful training and added experience finally paid off for Denis Hulme. In 1966 Brabham won the World Championship for the third time; the following year, the champ was Denis Hulme. It was only natural that McLaren and Hulme should strike out on their own.

Once they got started, there was no stopping them. In 1967 McLaren was the Can-Am champ. The following year it was Hulme, winning four of the (then) six races, in the bright orange M8A McLaren car. In 1969 there were eleven Can-Am events and McLaren won six of them.

The first race in the 1970 Can-Am series was scheduled to be run in mid-June. But even before the first Group 7 cars took off, the major burden of running Team McLaren fell on the shoulders of Denis Hulme. On June 2, while testing one of his cars at Goodwood, England, Bruce McLaren went off the road, crashed, and was killed.

The loss of Bruce McLaren was a staggering blow, but Team McLaren almost suffered a double loss. Only a few days before McLaren crashed, Hulme too was in an accident. In a practice session at Indianapolis, Denny had badly burned both hands. His left hand was bandaged for the next few Can-Am races, and his right hand showed angry red and mottled spots in several places.

Denis Hulme took over the front-line Team McLaren car. It was the one his boss would have used. But the number four on it—McLaren's number—was removed from the bright orange car, not to be used again. And to replace himself, Hulme persuaded his old friend, Dan Gurney, to come back to Team McLaren, at least for a while. In the past, McLaren and Hulme had often finished 1–2 in the Can-Am races. Now, it would be Hulme and Gurney.

The first scheduled race was at Mosport Park outside Bowmanville, Ontario (Mosport is a contraction of the words "motor sport"). It was then that the Can-Am's first fatality occurred. In practice, Dick Brown, a forty-year-old salesman from Michigan, went off the track at Turn 6 and crashed into an embankment.

Gurney and Hulme were 1–2 in qualifying for pole position. Gurney, tooling around the 2.459-mile lap, set a new track record of 1 minute 18.8 seconds, or an average speed of 116.72 miles per hour. The next day, as 30,000 fans watched, the cars took off on the 197-mile race.

For forty-four laps it was Gurney and Hulme leading the way. Suddenly, Jackie Oliver in an Autocoast Ti-22 Chevvy roared in between them and took over the lead. Hulme, fighting the pain that made it an effort to hold the wheel, waved to Gurney as if to say, "Go get him, Dan." Gurney blasted after Oliver and caught him on the sixty-first lap. His McLaren M8D was too much car for Oliver's Chevvy to catch. The race was over in 1 hour 47 minutes 56 seconds. Gurney had averaged 110.214 mph. Oliver was second. Hulme, despite the pain in his hands, managed to come in third.

Hulme and McLaren weren't angry at Oliver because he had passed them cleanly. But a feud was shaping up between Oliver and another Team McLaren driver, Lothar Motschenbacher. In the Mosport race the two had literally run into each other. Oliver claimed that Motschenbacher was guilty of "dirty driving." He said that Motschenbacher had slewed all over the track, refusing to let him pass. In desperation, Oliver had practically climbed all over Motschenbacher in the McLaren car, shoving it off the track and out of the race. Later, both drivers were officially reprimanded. Oliver was fined $50, Motschenbacher was not fined.

Race number two in the Can-Am series was held at Mont Tremblant, Quebec, a 2.56-mile track stuck away in the beautiful Laurentian Mountains, ninety miles north of Montreal. Racing fans had a double reason for turning out in large numbers; not only were they anxious to get a look at these fast Group 7 cars, but also to find out how Motschenbacher and Oliver would go at each other.

As it turned out, all Oliver did was go out of the race, but it wasn't because of anything Motschenbacher did. The Autocoast Ti-22 Chevvy was made partly of titanium, a light but strong metal. And that structure proved all over again that the chassis of a Group 7 car could be overpowered by its engine.

Oliver was tearing around the track in fine style when he went over a hill rise at 145 miles an hour. That was just a little too fast. The car wasn't heavy enough to take a quick "up-and-over" at such speeds. The Autocoast Ti-22 Chevvy went into the air like a plane, flipped over, and skidded along upside down. And Oliver walked away from that spill unhurt!

Gurney won the 198.5-mile race with an average speed of 99.95 miles per hour. Motschenbacher was second. Hulme didn't finish. Actually, Hulme ran the fastest lap in the race at 101.71 mph, but an overheating engine forced him out on the fiftieth lap. Team McLaren left Canada with two first places in two races. Next stop, Watkins Glen.

This great track in the Finger Lakes region of central New York State had had an in-and-out existence. Originally, it was a 6.6-mile series of steep climbs and drops, some oiled sections of road, and an underpass through a railroad trestle where no passing was allowed. Drivers considered it tough, but no better and no worse than a lot of other courses. However, crowd control along the public roads was poor.

In 1952, a driver named Fred Wacker, driving an Allard, misjudged the turn on Franklin Street. He hit the curb and plowed into some spectators, killing a child, and badly injuring several other people. The accident was enough to stop the race.

New York State soon banned racing on state roads, especially after a similar tragedy occurred at Bridgehampton on Long Island not long afterward. For a time, road racing in New York State faced an uncertain future.

But, as had happened before (and would happen again)

the Air Force came to the rescue, offering airports and men so that road races could be held. Circuits were laid out in the roomy stretches between hangars and along runways. There was time to build new circuits in various parts of the state—indeed, in regions all over the country. Several books and racing magazines had called Watkins Glen "the cradle of post-war racing in the United States."

By 1970, when the third race in the Can-Am series was held, Watkins Glen was an established, famous circuit, calling itself "the home of American road racing." Even then it was still being improved, with new fences in several places, plus a new forty-foot scoreboard. Watkins Glen also featured many outstanding attractions. For example, on that weekend in mid-July, there would be a six-hour endurance race on Saturday, followed by the Can-Am on Sunday. The following week fans could see a race called the Trans-Am. And in October, the track would play host to a certified Grand Prix race.

There were a couple of oddities in the 1970 Can-Am. For one thing, there were five Group 5 cars entered, which had run in the six-hour grind the previous day. There was nothing new in the idea of a Group 5 car challenging a Group 7 car. In 1968 Dan Gurney himself had tried to beat Group 7 cars with a smaller but more maneuverable car; it didn't work. What was rare was the fact that these cars had taken such a beating the previous day and when the sun rose again they were back to take another pounding. Indeed, automobile engineering had made great progress!

Even more unusual was Jim Hall's entry, a new Chaparral 2J-GEV. The letters GEV meant "ground effects vehicle." A more popular name for the weird-looking car was "the vacuum cleaner."

Jackie Oliver's "airplane ride" off the road in the Mont Tremblant race was not an isolated incident. In fact that was why the "airfoil" fin at the rear of some sports cars had been installed, to keep the tail of the car down as much as possible. Jim Hall had attacked the problem from a different angle.

Inside the Chaparral's box-like body were two fans, driven by small snowmobile engines. The fans drew air from inside the car and pushed it out. Therefore, the atmospheric pressure was lower inside the car than the pressure outside. This was supposed to form a partial "vacuum effect" and exert a "down-force" on the car, enabling it to hold the road better.

Hall reasoned that he needed an outstanding driver to give his new car a proper ride, and he chose the Great Scot, Jackie Stewart. But Stewart had his doubts about the car. He wasn't crazy about the idea of an automatic transmission. Also, Jackie had to get used to the idea of working the throttle with his right foot and the brakes with his left foot. Besides, Jackie had been a Formula I Grand Prix driver almost all the time for the past few years. He had to feel his way back into a sports car all over again. But he agreed to give it a try.

The records show that Denis Hulme won the 200.1-mile, eighty-seven-lap race. His time was 1 hour 41 minutes 15 seconds, an average of 118.56 mph. Dan Gurney finished ninth. But, although the McLaren-Chevvy won, in many ways it was really a victory for Porsche. In second place was Jo Siffert driving a Porsche 917, followed by two similar cars. Fifth was Mario Andretti in a Ferrari 512S, then came another Porsche. All the Porsches had competed the day before. In fact seven of the first ten cars to finish had competed in the six-hour grind on Saturday.

As for the "vacuum cleaner," it was moving along in third place for a while, but had to come into the pit because one of the snowmobile engines failed. That put a bad strain on the brakes. The pit crew worked on the car for twenty-nine minutes. Stewart tried to get back in the race, but after three more laps he knew it was hopeless. The car just wasn't working right.

Yet that "blowing box" had the fastest lap time. It figured out to 125.84 miles per hour.

Dan Gurney had wanted to get out of the Can-Am for some time, and after Watkins Glen he left Team McLaren. Gurney was replaced by Peter Gethin, an English driver. But by then almost everyone was convinced that the McLaren-Chevvy was well nigh unbeatable, especially since some of the most dangerous competition was in some sort of difficulty. In the fourth race, the Klondike 200 at Edmonton, Canada, the Autocoast Ti-22 cracked up. The vacuum cleaner was still in the repair shop. Hulme and Gethin finished 1–2. In fact they were the only ones to complete all sixty laps.

Nor were things any different in the fifth Can-Am race. That was the Buckeye Cup, held at the mid-Ohio Sports Car Course in Mansfield, Ohio. With his hands improving daily, Denis Hulme drove a dandy race and won. He led all the way, setting a new course record of 95.184 miles per hour. The old record had been set only the previous year—by none other than Denis Hulme. In second place was Peter Revson, driving a Lola T-220 Chevvy. He was a full minute behind, meaning Hulme beat him by about a mile and a half.

Race number six at Elkhart Lake, Wisconsin, should have been won by Hulme. He did come in first, but was disqualified, and the victory taken away.

On corner 5, a sharp left turn at the end of a fast straightaway, the car in front of Hulme spun out. Hulme also spun out in order to avoid a crack-up. A group of people standing by offered to give the stalled car a push in order to get it going again. Hulme started the car by "popping"—the same way any car with a standard gear-shift transmission can do it. The car is put in gear and the clutch pressed down, then people try to shove it as fast as possible. When the car has gained some speed, the clutch is let out suddenly. The car coughs, jerks, and the engine starts.

But the officials said that was illegal. The new winner was Bob Bondurant in a Lola-Chevvy. Bondurant had come out of retirement just for the Can-Am.

The seventh race had been scheduled for Bridgehampton, Long Island. But rainstorms had washed out the course some time before. Also, the track was having financial difficulty. The schedule was changed and *Road Atlanta* was substituted.

Road Atlanta was a brand new circuit, built at Gainesville, Georgia. It cost $1,300,000. The circuit was very beautiful, running through serene woods and grassy meadows for two and a half miles. There were eleven turns, and the longest straightaway was 4,300 feet. That was long enough for a car to rev up to 200 miles per hour.

When the race was all over, the circuit looked more like a track for a demolition derby than a race course. Had it not been so costly, it would have been funny. Someone remarked that it would not take many more crack-ups to turn the circuit into an auto graveyard.

Jim Hall's vacuum cleaner was back in action, but now it was in the hands of a driver named Vic Elford. Jackie Stewart had returned to Grand Prix racing. Elford, a very good driver, leaped into the lead, but had to fall back very soon because of those snowmobile engines. This time they developed ignition trouble.

Hulme took over the lead for ten laps. Then he got careless. A slower car (not all the entries were Group 7) was in front of him. Hulme was about to gain a full lap on the car driven by Gary Wilson. But Hulme misjudged Wilson's speed and rammed into the back of his car. Hulme's front end was badly crumpled.

Gethin took over the lead. Suddenly, two cars in front of him collided as he was about to gain a lap. Trying to avoid the crack-up, Gethin veered away and hit a retaining wall. The nose of Gethin's car was banged up, but not as badly as Hulme's.

Pure luck prevented a possible fatal accident. For no apparent reason Peter Revson spun out. Quickly, he got out of the car to see what was wrong. Revson got away just in time, for Bob Brown rammed into the stopped car broadside.

Soon, after quick repairs, Gethin was back in the race. He regained the lead. Then, with eighteen laps to go, his door came loose. Gethin went back to the pit to have it fixed. He started out again, but was flagged back because the officials said he had left the pit too soon. Gethin did it all over again. But in his anxiety to make up lost ground he revved his engine too much on a turn and broke the gearbox.

Who finally won Road Atlanta? A thirty-eight-year-old used car dealer from England, named Tony Dean. It was a case of good luck helping an unknown driver defeat the great drivers and faster cars. Dean had bought the 3-liter Porsche 908 second-hand. He had no sponsor and had to use his own money. Dean had been hoping to hang on long enough to finish a few races so that he could collect some purse money.

In second place was Dave Causey in a Lola-Chevvy. Third was Motschenbacher in the McLaren car. Good old Lothar! He had run in every Can-Am race since it began in 1966!

Race number eight was held at Donnybrooke Speedway in Brainerd, Minnesota. Peter Revson won the pole position, but in the race itself it was Denis Hulme the winner, Peter Gethin behind him, and Revson third. Denny had gone into the lead and nobody ever got ahead of him. He ran the 210-mile circuit in 1 hour 47 minutes 10 seconds, or 117.57 mph. Gethin was a minute slower.

Hulme did not win pole position in the number nine race at Monterrey. Vic Elford, in the vacuum cleaner, had that honor. But in the practice session before the race, he blew the engine. Good-bye vacuum cleaner for that race. Hulme won the 152-mile event with an average speed of 104.107 mph. Jackie Oliver was second, Peter Revson third again, and Chris Amon fourth.

Finally it was the beginning of November, time for one more race and then the 1970 Can-Am series would be history. The cars assembled at Riverside, California, to go around the 3.2-mile course.

Again that crazy Chaparral vacuum cleaner had the best qualifying time, 128.446 miles per hour. But it didn't mean a thing. Elford ran the car two laps and was forced into the pits. Out came the car, then it went back in again. The car just quit. Denis Hulme went on to win the unexciting race. His total time was nowhere near the time of the vacuum cleaner's best qualifying lap. Hulme averaged 120.284 miles per hour. Jackie Oliver was not far behind him.

There had been ten races in the 1970 Can-Am series. McLaren-Chevrolet had won eight of them, with Denis Hulme personally accounting for six victories. But Hulme and Gurney and Gethin and Motschenbacher were the first to acknowledge that their good showing was due to the fact that they were driving great cars. Even though he was no longer living, Bruce McLaren had given them the victory.

As for Jim Hall's vacuum cleaner, it raced no more. The McLaren Team (and many other manufacturers) had lodged a protest against the car. The CSI declared the Chaparral 2J illegal "because it violated the rules governing movable aerodynamic devices." All Jim Hall had to show for his efforts was an outlawed car, along with a lot of bills for spare parts, tires, and fuel.

But men like Jim Hall and Carroll Shelby and Bruce McLaren have advanced car design by giant leaps. And that is really what auto racing is all about. Yesterday's dream cars are built today, so that the cars of tomorrow will be still safer, much stronger, and slightly faster than the cars of the past.

# 6 · Rallies

Sometimes the word is spelled "Rally." But in many places, particularly in Europe, it shows up as "Rallye." Both are correct. No matter how it is spelled, a Rally (or Rallye) is a race which is not won by the swiftest, but by the most accurate.

When Rally officials plot a course, they decide on the time it should take to cover the distance between two points. If their decision makes the time sixty-five minutes, then that is the mark other drivers must equal. It doesn't matter whether the distance to be covered is twenty miles or fifty-five miles; the car coming closest to that particular time gets the points. That is what a Rally is all about. If there is one single word to describe this type of race, it is *control.*

The great Rallies can cover thousands of miles, so control demands split-second precision and timing over each marked-out section of the course. And sometimes even small computers, fancy odometers, and other complicated gadgets won't help. A great deal depends on two factors which cannot be controlled by man. The first factor is the weather, including rain, snow, high winds, bitter cold, or steamy heat. And that leads to the second factor: road conditions.

Slide rules are useless in a storm when a snow slide has

blocked the road. A huge hidden rock, lying under a layer of snow and slush, can break an axle easily. Or a dusty, hot jungle road can become a river bed when flash rainstorms strike.

Any youngster with a vivid imagination who has pictured himself in the role of a jungle explorer, would find his dream come true in the East African Safari. Or, if he (or she) has visions of becoming a mountain climber forcing a path through cold and snow, then the Monte Carlo Rallye would be ideal. But for normal adults, faced with a drive over those two courses, each one is a special nightmare.

The East African race takes four days and covers 3,100 miles. It runs through three countries: Kenya, Tanzania, and Uganda. The roads wind through bush country, jungles, swamps, and high hills. The course goes around a section of Lake Victoria, doubles back down south, then over to the Indian Ocean and back to the starting point, which is Nairobi. Along the way, the track leads through towns and villages with such names as Kakamega, Kampala, Mbale, Kitale, Nanyuki, Meru, back into Nairobi, then down to Mbulu, Kolo, Dar es Salaam, back up through Korogwe and finally to Nairobi. The driver and his navigator will certainly learn African geography, if nothing else.

On the average, less than ten percent of the starting cars finish the race. To understand what can happen, let us follow the 1963 winners, driver Nick Nowicki and navigator Paddy Cliff, as they overcame the perils of the Safari in their Peugeot 404.

It was early evening on April 11 when Nowicki and Cliff left the ramp in Nairobi. For a time all went well as they passed the checkpoints. It was near Kakamega, about 250 miles from Nairobi, that all the eighty-four cars in the event ran into difficulty. A long stretch of road had been turned into a rain-soaked quagmire. Everywhere, cars were mired axle-deep in mud, blocking passage through.

There was no time to put on chains. Paddy Cliff got out of the car, stepped up on the rear bumper, and began to bounce up and down. His weight gave the rear wheels extra traction. Meanwhile, Nowicki maneuvered to the edge of the road. Churning along the mud and grass of the shoulder, he weaved his way around the stuck cars.

One of the toughest pieces of driving consisted merely of trying to pass a Ford Cortina. It was dark, the road was still muddy, and speed limits were optional on that stretch. The Cortina went squishing along at 70 miles an hour. When the Peugeot got too close, splashes from the Cortina's rear wheels sent gobs of mud onto the Peugeot's windshield, and the wipers could not get it all off. It wasn't until much later that this particular Cortina was overtaken.

In an ordinary race, whether it is Grand Prix, endurance, or any other type, one of the "no-nos" is getting out and pushing the car when it gets stuck. In a Rally it's practically part of the contest. Local people even pick up some spare money helping racers shove their cars around rock slides or out of mud holes.

Nowicki and Cliff parted with numerous coins while getting up and over Mount Elgon, on the Kenya-Uganda border. Again the road was wet. Again cars were mud-mired all over the narrow road. Eager observers lined up along the course. They went dashing over to give a car a few hard pushes, accepted payment, then ran back to see who else needed help.

Always, the contestants were faced with the necessity of staying within the local speed limits. Sometimes they didn't make sense. For instance, it was all right to rev up the engines on the Nandi Hills Escarpment, moving through blinding rains, over rutted roads, at an average speed of 53 miles an hour. But at the Nakuru control point, a much safer area, cars slowed to 30 miles an hour, because that was the local speed limit. Anyone caught going faster would be penalized 100 points, the same as one hour and forty-five minutes in time.

When Safari officials learned that one ninety-mile stretch of road with ninety-two hairpin turns was washed out by a blinding rain, they changed the course. They wanted no fatal accidents on that ninety-mile stretch of course. Another route was chosen. It wasn't much better, but at least cars could get through.

At five o'clock in the morning, on April 13, the Peugeot pulled into Nairobi, the halfway mark. Nowicki and Cliff reported in and went to sleep. At four o'clock in the afternoon they were on their way again.

Try to imagine a road with ruts one-and-a-half feet deep. Add mud. Wash away part of the road. Put in some fog, to cut visibility down to about five yards. Drop some huge boulders along the way. And that is what the 140-mile stretch along the Mbulu section was like. Nowicki and Cliff made it.

On and on went the Peugeot. Nowicki and Cliff spoke idly about the flocks of wild game which they saw around the Morogoro crater. They held their breath when a tire blew out while they were clipping down a rock-filled road at 65 miles an hour. Not only was the tire shredded, but the wheel was also ruined. They threw both away, put on the spare, and continued on.

Through it all, no matter what the weather was like, no matter how bad the road, the driver and his navigator had to try to maintain the average speed set by the officials. There were several hairy moments.

The Peugeot was halted at one spot where the road dipped down and was completely underwater. How deep was it? What was the road bed like under the drifting water? There was only one way to find out. Nowicki shoved the car into first gear and edged in gingerly. The water went up over the hood and as high as the windshield. Desperately, Nowicki kept his foot jammed on the accelerator. The rugged Pugeot kept sliding through like a half-submerged motorboat. It chugged out of the water and onto "dry" (really muddy) road.

On another occasion even the daring Nowicki refused to take a chance. They stopped at a stream which had to be forded. The water rushed by like a flood at its crest. Blocking the road was an uprooted tree that had been swept there by the raging current. Nowicki tried to edge into the water. He felt the current begin to sweep the car sideways. Immediately, he threw it into reverse and got the car out just in time! Then he drove around in the dark, his bright headlights beaming ahead, until he found a more suitable spot to cross.

Further along the way another tire blew out. For fifteen minutes driver and navigator knelt in the pouring rain, tools, nuts, and bolts slipping out of muddy fingers as they changed the wheel.

And finally they drove triumphantly into Nairobi. They had won. Their nearest rival was seventy-five minutes behind, way off the mark.

The 1963 race was more or less typical of the East African Safari. The mud, the rushing waters, the rocks, the mountains, the accidents, were all part of it. Still, some of those elements could happen even on a Grand Prix course. But where else would a car be demolished because it smashed into a giant anteater at 70 miles an hour? Where else would a noisy helicopter be used to drive away the lions and elephants which were blocking the road? Where else would angry people line the road, throwing rocks at passing cars? (That happened in the Kilimanjaro section in 1964. Three drivers were injured. No one stopped to ask why the people were angry.)

It remained for *Time* magazine to give the best description of this great Rally: "If there were a Society for the Prevention of Cruelty to Automobiles, there would be no East African Safari!"

## THE MONTE CARLO RALLYE

It is a far cry from torrential rains, to driving sleet and snow; from strength-sapping heat and chill and damp night air, to temperatures that dip below freezing and stay there. That is the difference between the East African Safari and the Monte Carlo Rallye.

The Safari is comparatively new. It was inaugurated in 1953 in honor of Queen Elizabeth II's coronation. The Monte Carlo Rallye was first held in 1911, and is part of racing tradition. It has been called "one of the most important events of the winter season."

Automobile manufacturers know full well how important it can be to win the Monte Carlo Rallye. There is great prestige in a victory. So they overlook no detail when preparing for the event. For example, in 1965, BMC entered five cars. Knowing how difficult the course was, and that there might be a lot of ice and snow along the roads, the company made ready more than 500 extra tires. Some of the tires were studded with traction spikes.

The drivers paid as much attention to details as the manufacturers. They studied the route very carefully. Actually, the Rallye was divided into three sections: the various starting points, the middle of the race, and then the final section. It worked like this:

Each of the 237 entries chose one of nine different starting points. They could begin from Lisbon, from Paris, from Athens, and even from Minsk, Russia. It was up to the drivers to decide which one would be best for them. Each course on that first leg was approximately 2,400 miles, and had to be covered at an average speed of 31 miles an hour. The end of that leg—the first assembly point—was St. Claude, a small French town in the eastern Jura Mountains, near the Swiss border.

From there they would all travel through mountain passes and along mountain roads down to Monte Carlo.

The third and final part of the Rallye was "Monte Carlo to Monte Carlo," a route through the lower Alps.

Naturally, at all times, traffic and speed regulations had to be obeyed. To be stopped for speeding, or for any other infraction of local laws, meant disqualification.

In mid-January, all cars left their starting points. Very little of interest happened in the first phase. Nearly all made it safely to St. Claude.

Winter nights are long in the mountains. The Rallye officials had decided that the 550-mile stretch between St. Claude and Monaco was to be made at night. This section also included some high-speed roads, running through dangerous passes. It was a twisting course, generally southward. It ran through Chambery, a town called Gap, and then took a southeast swing to Monaco.

When the second part of the Rallye started it began to snow. But the snowfall was light and gentle at first. About one-third of the cars had passed through Chambery when the full fury of the storm struck. Between St. Claude and Chambery, over one-and-a-half feet of snow covered the roads. The storm worsened and visibility was cut. It was impossible to see more than five or six yards ahead. Yet the cars had to keep moving in order to maintain the timing set for the race.

Many cars were eliminated by the storm, including some of the favorites. All three of the Ford Mustangs which were entered had to quit, one of them with a broken wheel. A Saab, driven by the 1962 Monte Carlo Rallye winner, Eric Carlsson, lost valuable time because the carburetor froze. Paddy Hopkirk, the 1964 winner, hit a rock that was buried in the snow, snapping off a supporting front tie rod bracket from his BMC-Cooper.

A Finnish driver named Timo Makinen, also driving a BMC-Cooper, put on a fantastic show in the five speed stretches. Rounding dangerous turns, zipping through snow-covered passes—and praying a lot, too—he piled up valuable points. Three times he won a particular section, coming closest to the time mark. Once he was second. Once he was fifth.

Only thirty-five cars made it through to Monaco. The rest were strung out along the mountain roads, out of the race. It wasn't always the driver's fault, nor was there anything wrong with their cars. Sometimes the cars in front of them stalled out on the narrow roads, and it was impossible to go around until it was too late to reach the next checkpoint on time. Accidents, frozen parts, broken wheels, and axles accounted for many other dropouts.

On the final leg of the Rallye, Monte Carlo to Monte Carlo, other cars fell by the wayside. Paddy Hopkirk's hastily repaired car was one. The BMC mechanics performed a near-miracle, welding a whole new bracket on the car. He was given four new tires and sent away. But the bracket broke again and that was the end for him.

Lucien Bianchi in a Citroen had started the final leg of the race in second place. His studded tires were worn down and he was running out of gas. When he came to the next service point, Bianchi found to his dismay that the crew had moved somewhere else and he couldn't find them. Tired but determined, he set out for the next stop. But now the traction on his tires was gone. On an ice-glassy road surface, while going at 60 miles an hour, he crashed head-on into a tree. He and his navigator were unhurt, but the car was demolished.

More bad luck dogged the Citroens. One car, driven by the team of Coltelloni and Marang, roared into a blind curve at 70 miles an hour. It was almost a hairpin turn, and they had expected an easier, wider curve. The car sped completely off the road and flipped into the bottom of a thirty-foot-deep ravine. Both men were hurt, but fortunately, they recovered fully.

An odd sort of battle developed between Eric Carlsson and his wife, Pat Moss-Carlsson. Eric had managed to edge back up in the standings, from thirty-sixth place to sixteenth. But Pat in her Saab was ahead and her husband never did catch her. She finished third and won the women's prize handily. Pat had also been in the East African Safari and had made a creditable showing.

Timo Makinen won the Rallye. He took five of the six Monaco-to-Monaco speed sections, averaging close to 60 miles an hour on one of them. That particular stretch happened to be packed with snow from one end to the other.

Rallies can be fun when they are not too difficult. Some good amateurs have entered and taken prizes, but not in the East African Safari, and not at Monte Carlo either. Only the hardiest, the most knowledgeable, precision drivers and navigators can get through the championship Rallies of today.

This, then, has been a small visit to the world of auto racing. It is far from complete. Dozens of books such as this one would be needed to tell of all the Grand Prix races, all the sports car events, the Rallies, the hillclimbs, stock car races, sprint cars, and the various formula events. All are important.

Nor can one book do justice to the magnificent drivers who risk their lives to get around a course a second or two faster than before. They race because they love fast driving, because that is what they know how to do best. And they know that it can be richly rewarding insofar as money and fame are concerned.

The designers and manufacturers also deserve their share of the credit. Designers dream and plan, and try to find new ways to build safe, fast cars. Manufacturers invest millions of dollars in those dreams.

In the end, the beneficiaries are the people who drive automobiles. For all those races are testing grounds for new products, for better tires, and more rugged engines.

And besides, those races are such great entertainment for sports fans!

# Index

# About the Author

HOWARD LISS is a well-known and well-read author of many sports books for young people, among them several in Random House's *Punt, Pass and Kick Library*, plus books written in collaboration with many great athletes, such as football's Y. A. Tittle, baseball's Willie Mays, and Olympic silver-medal winner Penny Pitou. He has also written books on soccer, lacrosse, and basketball.

A writer since radio days, Mr. Liss once wrote gags for such comics as Jimmy Durante, Ed Wynn, Al Jolson, Jack Haley, and several syndicated comic strips. Always an avid sports fan, he recalls with splendor the details of games past, in books on baseball, football, basketball, and hockey. He has a fine ability to entertain sports fans with his own kind of "instant replay."

Mr. Liss's two daughters, teen-agers Jodi and Dana, keep him constantly in touch with young people. He makes his home in New York City.